Where there's a Will, there's a way

The remarkable life story of Will Crooks MP

Jim Crooks

Copyright © 2012 by Jim Crooks

All rights reserved.

ISBN:10: 1470162350
ISBN-13: 978-1470162351

This book is dedicated to my wonderful daughter, Ellie, who lights up my life every day.

To my wife, Tamara.

To my brother, Pete.

It is also dedicated to the memory of George Haw, who over a century ago gave us a personal insight into Will while he was still alive, while also recounting events from Will's childhood; events which would ultimately shape the man that became Will Crooks. Without George Haw, this book would not be possible.

And of course to Will himself, for even today making a difference in so many people's lives, whether they realise it or not.

Acknowledgements

Excerpts taken from the East London Advertiser reproduced with their kind permission.

Parliamentary speeches: Contains Parliamentary information licensed under the Open Parliament Licence v1.0.

Excerpts taken from the Municipal Journal reproduced with their kind permission.

Press release from the Stevedore Union reproduced with the kind permission of Unite (Transport and General Workers Union).

Notes

I have seen it reported across the internet that Will's mother's name was Charlotte. Even George Haw referred to her as Charlotte. However, in researching my family tree, I obtained a copy of Will's birth certificate and it plainly says there that Will's mother's name was Caroline, so that is what I'm using in this book. Also, the place of birth is listed as 1 Shirbutt Street on that certificate and not number 2 as is often quoted.

The spelling used in this book is British English.

INTRODUCTION

"Will Crooks is a Londoner straight out of Dickens. He was probably as close to becoming an organic labour leader as England has come. Distinct from almost all other Labour MPs, Crooks stood out as a representative that represents."

Ben Tillett, leader of the Great Dock Strike of 1889.

"No man of his time did more to awaken the conscience of the nation upon social conditions; he pleaded the cause of the poor on all manner of platforms, as well as in Parliament."

R. Clynes MP

Part 1

CHAPTER 1

The River Thames, Poplar, East London, England. 1855

The small, thin figure of George Crooks walked through the cold morning fog towards the wharf where the ship on which he worked as a stoker was moored. The collar of his dark shabby coat was upturned to keep out the morning chill. The fog was a blessing; it hid the squalor that was most of Poplar. It could not, however, hide the wretched stench of the River. As he walked past the ships that were docked there, he managed to sidestep a group of rats, which scurried away as he disturbed their foraging. He watched them as they disappeared back into the fog. The rats were an ever present resident of the docks because of the ample, easy food pickings found there. Even at this time of the day the river was noisy with the sound of warning bells, fog horns and the shouts of men.

He climbed the damp, wooden gangway that led to the steamer on which he worked, his heavy boots announcing his arrival on board. He waved across to the dimly lit figure of the night watchman sitting in the wheelhouse. The night watchman returned the wave and opened the door to the wheelhouse and leant out. He was a heavy set, pale faced man with a wisp of blond hair sticking out from beneath the front of his dark woolen hat.

"You're early today, George!" he called. "What's up?"

"Noisy engine yesterday," replied George. "I've come in early to give it a good oiling."

The night watchman shivered. "It's a chilly one this morning. I'm going back inside. Be careful around that engine now," he warned.

"I will," said George as he made his way across the deck to where the steps that led below deck were. At the bottom of the steps a young lad was already hard at work scrubbing the floor on his hands and knees. His clothes were nothing more than rags. He looked up when he saw George, exertion making his cheeks glow in the lamplight. "You're early today, Mr. Crooks," he said, smiling.

"Morning John," George answered, trying to avoid the area that was being scrubbed. "I've got an engine to oil."

"Oh," said John. "I don't envy you, Mr. Crooks, having to put your hands into all that machinery; sounds a bit dangerous to me."

"Just as long as I don't accidentally turn the engine on, I'll be fine," George laughed. John laughed too, although uneasily, and went back to work scrubbing the floor.

John was a good, honest lad, and he continued to scrub hard. The time passed. His vigorous scrubbing stopped mid-stroke as the engines started and a terrible scream echoed through the lower deck. He dropped his scrubbing brush and spun around facing the direction of the engine room, a look of terror distorting his young face. He could feel his heart pounding in his chest. He wanted to run to the engine room and help, but fear had him in its grip and it would not release him. He had to do something, he knew that, but going into the engine room wasn't an option. A vision of the night watchman flashed before him. "Of course!" he cried. He turned and ran up the steps taking two at a time and ran across the deck to the wheelhouse.

"Mr. Roberts!" he yelled at the watchman. "It's Mr. Crooks! I think there's been an accident!"

The watchman ran to the steps that took him below deck. John followed nervously. When they entered the engine room they found George on the floor lying on his side in a pool of blood.

"George!" shouted the watchman. There was no answer. He rolled George over onto his back. Horror spread across his face. "Oh my god! Where's his arm? John, go get help, now!" But the young lad did not move. His traumatised gaze was fixed on the engine mechanism and the mangled arm that hung there.

"John!" the watchman shouted again urgently. His shout brought the young lad back to his senses somewhat and he managed to slowly pry his eyes away and look down at the bloody figure that was George.

"John!" the watchman snapped. "You need to go and get help, NOW!" John finally nodded, turned and ran for help.

2

George Crooks had married Caroline Elizabeth Coates back in 1847. They had five children. The three eldest; Richard, Ann and three year old, Will, huddled together on their box bed, which they all shared in their one bed-roomed home at number 1 Shirbutt Street in Poplar, East London. The box bed, named because it resembled a large wooden box, had two wooden ends (head and feet ends) that were connected on top by a wooden ceiling panel. Its two open sides had curtains hanging from the ceiling panel to prevent draughts and also for privacy. The mattress on which the children slept was made of straw. The rest of the room was poorly furnished. There was one large window divided into four wide rectangular panes through which the overcast day outside spread its gloom into the Crooks family's troubled home.

Will, along with his siblings watched intently as their mother carefully changed their father's bandages, where until recently his arm had been joined to his shoulder. They sat and watched in silence; fascinated, yet horrified at the disabled figure of their father. Their mother was a strong woman. She needed to be. She was also loyal, and she loved her family dearly. The accident had now had time to sink in and she was under no illusions as to how hard their lives were about to become. There would not be much work to be found for a one armed ship's stoker. As a mother to five children, a nurse to her husband and now the main bread winner, she knew that life for her in particular would be the hardest of all.

As time passed and their father's health improved, he tried desperately to find work, but the only employment that he could find was the occasional job of watchman. Money became scarce. Caroline was a seamstress, and she now worked long hours into the night, sometimes even throughout the night. The children would often help her carry the clothes that she had made, mainly oil skin coats on foot to Houndsditch, a journey of approximately seven miles as they could not afford to pay for transport.

Will's eldest brother, Richard, also helped his mother in more than just the carrying of the clothes for her, for he began to help her with the sewing too and soon became as good with a needle as any seamstress. He too would often work through the night beside his mother to help her finish a job.

In the middle of the night, Will awoke and noticed the flickering of candlelight through a gap in the bed's curtain and realised he had been woken by the sound of crying. He sat up and pulled the curtain back. He saw his mother sitting alone crying as she sewed by candlelight.

"Why are you crying?" he asked her, keeping his voice low so he wouldn't wake the others.

"Never mind, Will boy," she replied sadly. "You go back to sleep."

"But you must be crying about something," he persisted.

In a rare moment of weakness, she cried, "It's through wondering where the next meal is coming from, my boy. Now go back to sleep before you wake everyone." He closed the curtain and lay back down and tried to sleep, but he couldn't. His young mind was puzzled and full of questions. "Why is she crying because she can't get bread? Why can't she get bread? I saw plenty in the shops yesterday. Do all mothers cry before they can get bread for their children?"

Boxing Day, 1856, Early Morning

When the children began to wake from their sleep, their mother, already dressed in her overcoat approached their box bed. "Now heed me," she said sternly. "I don't want any of you getting out of bed until I get back. Is that clear?"

"Where are you going?" Will's eldest brother Richard asked.

"Never you mind, my boy," she said. "Just do as I say."

The children knew better than to disobey her, so they stayed in their bed. Will didn't really mind that much. It was cold in the house and it felt good being under the covers enjoying the body heat of his siblings. He lay on the bed and turned his head to stare out of the window. His mother had opened the curtains before she left and Will looked out onto Shirbutt Street. It had snowed the day before and some of the snow still lay on the icy ground. He watched as people hurried by, bundled up as best they could against the freezing temperature. As the people passed by close to his window, Will could hear the faint crunch of ice under their feet. He wondered why his mother had to leave the house on a day like this.

At the top of the window he noticed a ragged row of small icicles hanging down from the grey bricks that overhung the window frame outside. He stared at them in wonder. As the morning wore on, he noticed small droplets of water begin to drip from the icicles, which then fell and hit the windowsill below and splashed lightly against the bottom panes. He moved up closer to the edge of the bed to get a better look, ignoring his siblings behind him as they became ever more restless and waited expectantly for the next droplet of water to fall. He wondered if his mother would return before the icicles melted completely. It seemed to him that she had been gone a long time already.

At last his heart leapt when he saw his mother pass by the window and then heard the door open. She looked frozen when she entered the room. She placed half a loaf of bread upon the table with an odd expression on her face that Will didn't quite understand, but then she turned and smiled at the children and told them that they could now leave their bed.

Later that day, George returned home after being out most of the day looking for work. When Caroline had to pop out to deliver some sewing work that she had completed, Will overheard his brother Richard telling their father how they had not been allowed to get out of bed earlier in the day. George looked down at his eldest son and said sadly, "After my accident your mother made a promise to herself that her children should never get out of bed unless there was some breakfast for them to eat." Will was too young to understand, but the odd expression on his mother's face from earlier in the day was a mix of determination and accomplishment. She had been able to keep her promise to herself for another day and had found enough food for her children for a meal, no matter how scant it proved to be.

When there was food in the house it was usually bread and treacle for breakfast, bread and treacle for lunch, and bread and treacle for dinner, all washed down with a glass of cold water. Sometimes if they were lucky, the treacle would be replaced by dripping, which is a type of fat used in cooking. However, there were plenty of times when there was neither treacle nor dripping to be had.

3

The gaunt, aging street vendor in his shabby frock coat and even shabbier top hat stood smiling a somewhat toothless smile through his unkempt greying beard at the passers-by. His once gold coloured cravat was now a dirty brown.

"Street ballads!" he called to advertise his wares. "Just a penny to fill your loved one's heart with music, sir!" he called as one particularly jolly looking gentleman strolled by; but the man just smiled back sweetly and kept on walking.

The vendor was having a slow sales day. The only thing he sold was the lyrics to popular street ballads. He'd had a fairly good day yesterday and sold several, but he'd been doing this long enough to know that a good day was often followed by a slow day, and of course, many days he didn't sell anything at all.

He heard a giggling in the distance and watched as a young couple approached. They looked like a typical young working class couple and both seemed like they had enjoyed more than a few gins between them. The man, wearing a flat cloth cap, dark trousers and a dark sack coat stopped abruptly in front of the vendor catching the giggling woman by surprise. She was dressed in a long green dress, which was narrow at the waist and then filled out into a loose bell bottom thanks to her crinoline underneath that gave it its shape. The dress had seen better days. Only when her companion stopped did she seem to notice the vendor for the first time.

"Sir, Madam," the vendor said smoothly, nodding slightly. "Could I interest you good people in one of these street ballads? I have both new and traditional."

"Do you have any of the new music hall songs?" the man asked.

"Alas sir, no. We're not allowed to sell them what with the copyright laws and all. The music halls are rather strict when it comes to making sure us street folk don't sell on any of their songs, if you know what I mean. I'm an old man, sir and don't want any trouble so I keep my nose clean." He lowered his voice. "However, sir, I do have a couple that are very similar to those latest music hall songs, but I'm afraid the lyrics may be a little too risqué for the young lady." The woman started giggling again at being referred to as a 'young lady'. Young she may be, she thought, but a lady? Just the same, she couldn't help but touch up her hair with her hand to make sure she was looking her best.

The young man stood thinking for a while, absentmindedly playing with his thick moustache, weighing up whether to risk losing his new lady friend if he seemed too cross. At last he decided to play it safe. "What else do you have that's popular?" he asked.

"The workhouse boy is a popular song, sir. It's said that not only is it based on a true story, but that Mr. Dickens himself was inspired to write Oliver Twist when he heard this song."

The man looked impressed.

"Really?" he asked

"Upon my honour, sir, that's what I've heard."

"How much is it?"

"Just a penny to you, sir, and that's a bargain if you ask me, what with its illustrious pedigree and all."

The man put his hand into his pocket to find a penny and the vendor's face lit up at the prospect of a sale, but the woman stepped in. "Aren't you going to listen to it first before you buy it?" she asked. It was her first contribution to the conversation and the vendor wished that she had kept quiet. If her companion didn't like it then he would lose the sale. "What a grand idea, Madam," he said through a forced smile. He took out the song lyrics and tried to clear his throat. On the third attempt at clearing the effects of the London smog from his throat he felt happy enough to begin.

"The cloth was laid in the workhouse halls,
the greatcoats hung on the whitewashed walls.
The paupers all were blithe and gay,
keeping their Christmas holiday.

    And we all of us say it and we say it with sneers;
    that Jamie's been murdered by the overseers

When the master he said with a murderous leer;
"You'll all get fat on your Christmas cheer."
And each by his looks he seemed to say;
"I'll have more soup on this Christmas day."

    And we all of us say it and we say it with sneers;
    that Jamie's been murdered by the overseers.

At length all of us to bed were sent,
a boy was missing and in search we went.
We sought him high and we sought him low,
we sought him with faces of grief and woe.

> And we all of us say it and we say it with sneers;
> that Jamie's been murdered by the overseers.

We sought him that hour and we sought him that night,
we sought him in fear and we sought him in fright.
When I heard a young pauper who then did cry;
"We'll all have to starve till we find that boy."

> And we all of us say it and we say it with sneers;
> that Jamie's been murdered by the overseers.

At length the soup copper repairs did need,
the coppersmith came and there he seed,
a pile of bones lay a-sizzling there,
and the leg of the breeches the boy did wear."

The couple stood wide eyed in shock for a moment, but then the woman spoke. "Buy it!" she said excitedly, "Go on, buy it!"

As the couple walked away with their street ballad lyrics in hand singing the song to themselves while the tune was still fresh in their heads, the vendor raised the coin to his lips and kissed it. It was another penny that put distance between he himself and the workhouse. He had been an inmate of that institution once before and he had no desire to return there. He knew its horrors.

1861

The years following George's accident have not been easy for the Crooks family. Will now has three brothers and three sisters and with the help of Parish out-relief, which his mother has pleaded for, they manage to survive. Parish out-relief was a small sum of money paid to some poor families under the Poor Law Act to aid them through hard times and to help them remain outside of the workhouse.

One morning a young boy walked along Shirbutt Street and stopped outside number 1. He reached up and took the heavy black cast iron knocker in his hand and gave two sharp knocks on the door. When Will's mother, Caroline, opened the door the boy respectfully removed his cap and asked, "Mrs. Crooks?"

"Yes, that's me," she said.

"I'm a messenger from the Poplar Guardians," he announced. The Poplar Guardians were the people in charge of the out-relief that the family was receiving. "I've been sent to tell you that you've been summoned to appear before the Guardians."

She knew in her heart that she was not being summoned to be given good news. She gathered up the children and walked to the building where the Guardians met. Once inside they were shown into a large room where the men that were the Poplar Guardians sat behind a long wooden desk. The room was simply decorated and behind these men hung portraits of Her Majesty Queen Victoria and her husband, Prince Albert. The frightened children clung timidly to their mother's skirt. The stern, emotionless faces of the Guardians only increased their fear.

The heavy set, balding man sitting in the middle of the row of Guardians in a larger, higher backed chair than the others was the chairman. His bushy sideburns stood out proudly on his age worn face; a face that looked as though it wore a permanent frown. He spoke in a loud, clear voice as he said, "Mrs. Crooks, you are here today because we need to review the out-relief that you have been receiving."

"Yes, sir," she replied, her voice shaking nervously. "We're very grateful for the help that you've given us. I don't know what would have become of us without it." He nodded his head slightly to acknowledge her thanks. His gaze then fell on the children. He singled out Will. With a long finger he pointed at him. "It's time that boy was getting his own living." Poor Will felt like running from the room as everyone's gaze fell upon him. He clung even tighter to his mother's skirt.

"He is at work, sir," his mother said, now finding a little courage after seeing her child singled out. "He gets up at a quarter to five every morning and goes around with the milkman for sixpence a week."

Will relaxed a little after his mother had defended him, but he was soon clinging tightly to her skirt again as the chairman demanded, "Can't he earn more than that?"

"Well, sir," she answered. "The milkman says he's a very willing boy and always punctual, but he's so little that he doesn't think he can pay him more than sixpence yet."

The chairman looked at his fellow board members. "Does anyone have any further questions?" The board members shook their heads to say, no, they had not. He turned his attention back to the family. As he clasped his hands and rested them on the heavy wooden desk in front of him, he said solemnly, "Mrs. Crooks, I'm afraid we cannot offer you any more out-relief. We can, however, take your children into the workhouse if you so wish."

"No!" was her anguished cry. "Is there really nothing else you can do for us?"

"I'm afraid not, Madam," said the chairman, his face set.

"Come along then children," she said proudly as she fought back tears. "Let's go home."

Without the help of the parish out-relief, the weeks that followed were very hard. It was a constant struggle to put bread into the mouths of the family. At last, in desperation, Will's parents agreed that five of the children, including Will, but excluding Richard the eldest and Walter who was only two should enter the workhouse. It was also agreed that Will's father, George, would be admitted too.

As they approached the grim prison like building and passed through the high black iron gate that led them into the courtyard, George tried his best to comfort the little ones, but as they crossed the cobbled courtyard and the wide, three storied grey mass of a building stood menacingly over them, they couldn't help but be terrified.

When they nervously entered through the main door to the Workhouse, they were met by the smell of tobacco smoke and a man that barely glanced up at them from his desk. The end of the pipe that was hanging from his mouth was hidden beneath his heavy moustache. A plume of pipe smoke rose as he opened his mouth to speak.

"Names and ages?" he asked, making no attempt to hide his boredom. He had asked that same question on so many other occasions when welcoming the borough's poor through those doors that he couldn't help but be bored.

"I'm George Crooks. Age 39. These are my children.

Ann. Age 11
Will. Age 9
Caroline. Age 7
Dorcas. Age 6
Robert. Age 4"

When the man had finished writing down their details, he picked up a large brass bell and gave three loud rings and then shouted, "Male and Female!" A door opened at the end of the short corridor and a male and female officer came through it and walked towards them. The female officer spoke first. "Girls, you'll come with me." The girls hesitated and looked up at their father as the officer turned and began to walk away. George nodded at the girls to let them know they should follow her. "Ann, take your sisters' hands. You'll need to look after them now until we get out of here."

"Yes, father," the girl answered sadly as she took her sisters' hands in hers and led them away. George's lip trembled as he watched his daughters being led away. He felt like wailing, but he knew he had to be strong for his children's sake. He cursed the day of the accident that had ultimately placed his family in such distress.

The male officer then spoke to George. "You and the boys will come with me." They followed the officer into a room where a large leather chair sat in the middle of it. The chair faced a large mirror on the wall. Regular chairs lined the walls and the officer pointed to those and said, "Take a seat there, the Barber will be along shortly."

"Why are we having our hair cut?" Will asked his father, but it was the officer that answered him.

"If you have head lice, getting rid of your hair will stop you giving them to others. It'll also stop you getting the little blighters while you're here. No hair means no lice."

When the Barber arrived, they one by one had their hair cropped short. Robert couldn't help but cry when he looked at the strange sight of his brother and father without their hair. When the Barber had finished with them, the officer led them into a large room with high white washed walls. "The doctor will come to see you," he said. "It might be a while though, so make yourselves at home."

There were wooden chairs scattered around the room, but George decided to sit on the floor with his back against the wall. The two boys sat on either side of him as close as they possibly could and here they stayed all night and most of the following day until the doctor arrived. After the doctor had checked them, they were finally led out into the main workhouse building. This time they were met by different officers. The new male officer spoke, "You need to come with me," he said to George. "The boys will need to go with Mrs. Jenks," he added, pointing to the female officer. Just like their sisters, the boys hesitated and looked up at George.

"Be brave boys," he told them. Will nodded, took Robert's hand and followed Mrs. Jenks.

"What are your names?" Mrs. Jenks asked.

"I'm Will and he's Robert."

She led them to a large washroom, inside of which were a line of rooms that held baths. She unlocked two of the doors to these rooms. Will was told to stand in one and Robert in the other. The officer ran the cold tap while two other women carried in pots of hot water that were added to the baths. When they were filled, Mrs. Jenks called over the officer in charge who placed a thermometer into the water to check that it was no colder than 90 degrees, or no hotter than 98 degrees. The boys were then stripped and bathed. Their clothes were taken away to be washed, disinfected, and then put into storage, only to be returned when it was time for them to leave the workhouse.

When they had been bathed and dried, they were issued with ill fitting workhouse uniforms, which Will at once found incredibly uncomfortable. Mrs. Jenks then led them out of the washrooms and took them to their dormitory. The long dark room had wooden beds lined up along both sides. Some children were sitting up on their beds talking, but most were just lying on them. Some were asleep, many lay crying.

"Can Robert share my bed?" Will asked, timidly.

Mrs. Jenks was a stern looking woman so when she looked down at Will, his first instinct was to turn away, but instead he held her gaze.

"Yes he can, lad," was the welcome reply. She showed them to their bunk and they laid down on the rough mattress; Robert in front of Will so that Will could cuddle and comfort his younger brother. Will pulled the blanket up to cover them both and there they lay. "I want to go home, Will," cried Robert softly. "Me too," sniffled Will. "Me too."

Will comforted his brother until he fell asleep, but his own thoughts were too active for sleep. He lay awake and thought of his mother. "What must she be thinking?" he asked himself. Here she was, a god fearing religious woman and regular church goer, and her only reward is to see her husband crippled and her children taken from her and put in the workhouse. His thoughts also drifted to his father and to his three sisters. He remembered the frightened looks on their little faces as they were led away. He prayed desperately that they would not be split up so that they would at least have each other for support.

His thoughts were interrupted by a boy a few beds away who started shouting all kinds of garbled nonsense in his sleep. The boy in the next bed rolled over and with the help of the moonlight shining in through the large bare windows saw Will awake in the darkness looking in the direction of where the shouting was coming from. "He's not all there," the boy whispered. "He's a bit mental."

"Oh," Will whispered back.

"It's like this every night," the boy sighed. He managed a slight resigned smile for Will's benefit and then closed his eyes and tried to go back to sleep. Will lay awake for hours listening to the strange babblings of the boy in the other bed. Interspersed among the babbling, Will could sometimes hear the boy cry out for his mother. Will felt like crying out for his too.

5

When Will awoke the next morning, his empty stomach growled because he was so hungry. He and Robert sat on their bed watching the other boys as they awoke and got themselves out of bed. The boy in the next bed that had spoken to Will the night before said, "Just follow everyone to the washroom. Once you've finished there, follow everyone to the dining room for breakfast." Will's spirits lifted at the thought of food. When they reached the dining room, Will and Robert lined up with the other boys, their faces, every one of them glum looking. When Will and Robert received their jugs of 'skilly' he understood why. Skilly looked to be nothing more than greasy hot water with a lumpy substance at the bottom. The lumpy substance was oatmeal.

Will led Robert to one of the long, bare wooden tables and sat down on the hard wooden bench. He took a mouthful of the skilly and promptly heaved. He thought for sure that he would be sick; it was disgusting. Robert did a little better and managed to drink some. Will, however, no matter how hard he tried, could not drink it. Every time he tried it made him feel sick to his stomach. "It's not something you get used to either," said the boy sitting next to him who went back to trying to swallow his. "Lunch is a bit better, but not by much," the boy added. "At least the bread is kind of edible."

A commotion broke out at the other end of the table and all the boys stood to see what was going on. Two boys were going at each other with fists flying and a male officer was trying to get in between them to break up the fight. "Sit down!" an officer that was standing close to Will's table roared. Everybody sat down at once, but they all still strained their necks trying to watch the fight. The two boys that were fighting were brought under control and Will and the other boys watched them as they were led out of the dining room. "They'll be in for it now," the boy sitting next to Will whispered.

"What will happen to them?" Will asked.

"They'll get a good caning, probably six of the best, locked away by themselves for a day and just fed bread and water."

Will's mouth fell open in horror. He was not used to such violence. "I'm glad I'm not a fighter," he said.

"You might have to fight while you're in here," the other boy told him.

"What if somebody tries to take your bread, or your brothers? You'll need to fight to stand up for yourself. If you do, just make sure you don't get caught."

Where there's a Will, there's a way

Will's heart sank. He had never had a fight in his life and he prayed that he would never have to. After breakfast, Will and Robert were directed to their respective school rooms. Because of the difference in age between them they had to be separated. Will followed the other boys in his age group in a daze. He was so hungry and now felt light headed from lack of food.

Will's school room had rows of wooden benches spread out from side to side, from the back of the room to the front. In front of the benches were lines of wooden desks. The desks faced the front of the room where the teacher sat to one side behind his own desk, which sat directly beneath one of the room's large windows. To his side, at the very front of the room stood a large blackboard.

Through the course of the day, the teacher, a stern looking, pale faced man with a bald head, long white beard and piercing eyes taught the boys lessons on reading, writing, adding, subtraction and Christianity. Even though the boys were all around the same age, they were all at different levels of their learning, so it was not an easy task for the teacher to keep on top of what was being taught. The only break came at lunchtime when Will got to eat some bread that was served with the revolting skilly. Again he was unable to drink that foul liquid, but he couldn't quite believe how good the stale bread tasted on his empty stomach. An added bonus that he wasn't prepared for was a piece of cheese. He almost cried with happiness at the sight of it. His spirits were also lifted when he saw Robert in the dining room too. He was grateful to be able to spend the short time before lessons again with his young brother.

After the day's lessons had been completed it was exercise time. The children were led out into a yard and Will fell in with the other boys as they walked around and around the yard in a large circle. After 15 minutes the call was given to fall out and the boys were given time to play before supper. Again, Will spotted Robert and together they sat on the ground with their backs to a wall; neither wanted to play and they hardly uttered a word. When they were brought inside for supper they were served bread, cheese and a small helping of mutton. Will went to bed still feeling hungry.

Day after day for three weeks this unchanging routine continued, each day feeling longer than the previous. None of the boys laughed much even when they were back in their dormitory and if they did they tried to keep the laughter down for fear of one of the officers hearing it and then being scolded for causing a disturbance.

At the end of their third week as they waited to leave the dining room one morning after breakfast, an officer called out a list of names; Will and Robert were on the list. "If your name is on that list, come and stand by me," the officer ordered. Will led Robert over to where the officer stood and joined the other boys that were gathering there. All looked as perplexed as Will felt. "Don't get excited," the officer told them. "You're not going home. There's an omnibus waiting outside that is going to take you to the Poor Law school in Sutton." When they climbed on board the omnibus, they saw that it was filled with a mixture of boys and girls, but unfortunately, his sisters were not among the passengers. When they sat down next to each other, Robert asked Will, "Where's Sutton?"

"I think it's on the other side of the river," Will replied. He was correct. Sutton lay some twenty-five miles away from their home. When they entered the school, hand in hand, the officer that greeted them asked, "Names and ages?" Will spoke for them both; "I'm Will, aged nine and my brother here, Robert, is four, sir." The officer pointed to a room. "You wait in that room; your brother will have to wait in the room next to it."

"Will we be allowed to stay together, sir, like back in the workhouse? He's only four!"

"Not here you won't boy; now move along," the officer said coldly. As Will led his brother by the hand towards the waiting room that the officer had indicated for Robert, he could feel his brother shaking as he sobbed at the news that they were to be separated. Will stopped at the door to the room, hugged Robert and kissed his smaller brother's forehead and tried to reassure him that everything would be all right. Will of course did not know if they ever would be, but he did his best to put on a brave face for Robert's sake. When a female officer in the waiting room saw them outside the door she came over to them. "So who do we have here?" she asked, her voice somewhat softer than that of the officer that they had just spoken to, although still very businesslike.

"His name's Robert!" said Will.

"Hello Robert!" the woman said to him as she held out her hand to take Robert's. "You come with me and we'll get you settled. You'll need to go into that waiting room," she told Will, pointing in the direction of the room. Will nodded and then watched them both turn around. He stared at their backs as they disappeared into their room. Will didn't know it then, but it would be the last time he would see Robert until the day they left the school together.

As Will entered his own assigned waiting room, he could do nothing to stop his own tears spilling. He knew that Robert was feeling scared and alone not knowing what was going to happen next, because Will himself was feeling exactly the same way.

When night time came, Will could not sleep. He thought of Robert, somewhere close by, but out of sight and reach. He remembered how he had had to comfort him at the workhouse to get him to sleep. How was Robert doing now? Was he sleeping, or lying awake scared and confused?

Where there's a Will, there's a way

Will could only toss and turn as his thoughts turned to the rest of his family. How he missed them all. The days were long, but the nights seemed endless and he soon became depressed. He could not stop worrying about his family. After a few days of being at the school, another boy approached him.

"Hello!" he said. "I hear you're a Poplar boy too."

"That's right, my name's Will." Will told him.

"I'm Henry!" the boy said, smiling.

"How long have you been here?" Will asked.

"Six months or so," the boy replied sadly.

Will's heart sank at the thought of being there for that long.

"How're you settling in?" the boy asked.

Will sighed, "Every day that I spend in this place is burnt into my soul."

"Ah," said Henry, gravely. "You just wait until Sunday. Every Sunday here is as long as a fortnight."

When Sunday did arrive, Will followed the other boys into the day room and found somewhere to sit. He soon realised what Henry had meant. From noon to 6 p.m. the boys were not allowed to play and their only entertainment was the clock and a window to look out of. Will, like many of the other boys spent the day staring out of the large window dreaming of the day when they would be reunited with their loved ones, if indeed the poor wretches had any. During the week after school hours the boys were allowed to use the playground, but Will had no desire to play. He spent the time in the playground by himself, sitting with his back against the wall, sad, lonely and depressed.

One day out of the blue as Will was eating his lunch, an officer at the school called out his name. Will jumped to his feet, startled. "Yes, sir!" he said, sounding alarmed, not knowing why he was being called upon.

"Go to the tailors shop after lunch and get your clothes," the officer ordered.

"What for, sir?" was Will's confused reply.

"You're going home, boy," said the officer.

Will practically fell back down into a sitting position onto the bench; he was stunned and his head reeled with excitement. Boys surrounded him, slapping him on the back and offering their congratulations, all wishing they were in Will's place. Will thanked them all. It was the first time that he had felt a smile on his face for so long, but inside he had nothing but pity in his heart for these poor souls that he would leave behind. As soon as lunch was over, Will headed for the tailors and changed back into his own clothes. At the gate he was met by young Robert, and even his sisters. He ran to them and threw his arms around each and every one of them and hugged them for all he was worth. They all cried, laughed and hugged, relieved that their nightmare was at last over.

As they journeyed back together in the omnibus to Poplar, they shared with each other their own recent personal journeys through the workhouse system. They were not happy tales.

Back at Poplar they were greeted at the workhouse gates by their mother. The children threw themselves into her outstretched arms and she comforted them like only a mother can. "Come on," she said at last. "Let's get you all home." As they started to walk away from the gates, Will asked, "Where are we going, this isn't the way home?"

"We've had to move, Will," she said sadly. "I've taken on more work to get you children home, but I've also had to get us a cheaper room."

"We don't mind!" Will said, "Just as long as we're all together and not in the workhouse. We're happy to live anywhere."

"Well I hope you still feel like that when you see where it is," she warned.

"Where is it?" he asked, a note of concern in his voice.

"It's in the High Street, Will, but it's right next door to the Workhouse casual ward." His heart sank at the mention of the workhouse and it was met by a chorus of worried mutterings from the other children. "What's a casual ward?" Will's eldest sister, Ann asked. Their mother explained. "The casual ward is a place where people usually stay just one or two nights at the workhouse. It's somewhere where somebody can get a meal and somewhere to sleep in exchange for working a set number of hours. We'll see a lot of people going in and out of there, but hopefully you children will never have to set foot in the workhouse again. I promise I'll do everything in my power for that never to happen again."

"Is Father out?" Will asked.

"Not yet Will, but we'll get him out soon."

As they approached their new home, Will saw with horror that it also backed onto the main workhouse building, the same building that until recently had been their temporary home. With the main workhouse building behind them and the casual ward to the side, he was to be reminded on a daily basis of the horrors of the Workhouse system. On the other side of the house stood a morgue, which might have usually unsettled any child, but Will knew that only what was in the workhouse could hurt him and not the morgue. He did not know it then, but this was to be his home for the rest of his boyhood.

6

March, 1863

Will often tried to bring a little extra money into the home by mudlarking down by Limehouse Causeway with his friends. Mudlarking involved waiting for the tide to go out and then climbing down into the muddy banks of the Thames to scour through the mud and grime for anything of value that they could sell, usually to the 'rag-and-bone' man.

On this particular day, Will and his friends removed their shoes, socks and shirts, keeping just their short trousers on as they climbed carefully down the old wooden ladder to the smelly grey mud below. Will's feet disappeared straight away up to his ankles. "Yuck!" he cried as the cold mud covered his feet.

"Stop whining, Will, and get out of the way so we can get down too," one of his friends shouted from the ladder. The mud was loose enough that Will could free his feet easily and he sludged on ahead of his friends looking for anything of value that caught his eye.

"That thing is huge!" said one of his friends as he nodded in the direction of a huge hulk moored close by. A hulk is a ship that is afloat, but incapable of going to sea. They were usually used for prison ships, or before that, for temporarily holding many people waiting to be transported to Australia and elsewhere overseas.

As the boys moved along the muddy banks of the Thames and got closer to the hulk, they could see that the deck was covered with many men in uniform. They could also see large groups of these men beginning to leave the hulk laughing and joking as they made their way down the gangway.

As best they could, the boys hurried through the deep mud towards them shouting 'Hello!' and waving their arms frantically to get the men's attention. Some of the men waved back laughing and threw coins down for the boys to scramble after. The coins promptly disappeared into the mud as soon as they landed, but these boys were eagle eyed. They scrambled over to where the coins had made tiny holes on impact and managed to claw through the mud to retrieve them. It was a messy, but successful day's mudlarking.

Later that day, back at home, Will and his family were disturbed by a commotion coming from outside in the street, so they went out to investigate. A number of open carts had been parked on the street, some of them right outside Will's house. A large number of policemen and a growing number of curious neighbours were beginning to gather around them. Right next door to Will's house was the morgue and it was obvious from the covered shapes on the back of the carts that their cargo was meant for there.

One of Will's neighbours, a friend that was with him earlier down in the causeway came running over when he saw Will. "Will! Have you heard the news?" he asked wide eyed. "There was a mutiny on that big hulk we saw down on the causeway today."

"What hulk?" Will's father asked.

Before Will could say a word, his excited friend told the whole Crooks family everything he knew. "We saw a huge hulk today moored at the causeway. Apparently it's called 'Venus' and we saw lots of men in uniform leaving the hulk and some of them threw coins into the mud for us. Well it seems those men were soldiers and they are just staying on the hulk while their frigate 'Arica' is being repaired." Barely taking a breath he added, "Apparently a lot of the soldiers went ashore and got drunk and when they went back on board later they refused to take orders. My father says there are 90 soldiers on board and 70 sailors. The drunken soldiers grabbed their muskets and bayonets and they tried to drive the sailors below deck, but a big fight broke out and some of the men were killed." Will and his family all looked aghast at the covered bodies on the back of the carts.

"Everyone back inside!" Will's mother ordered. "Quickly now, I think we've all seen enough here."

As they walked back inside the house, Will asked her, "Why do people get drunk? Those men seemed so happy when they were leaving the hulk today. Getting drunk seems like such an awful thing to do if it makes them act like that." Will was well used to seeing the drunks around the East End stumbling out of the pubs and becoming abusive and even violent. He just couldn't understand how people with so little money wasted so much of it on getting drunk if it made them act so badly. He looked up at his mother and waited for an answer, but on this occasion she had no answer for him. It was a mystery to her too.

It had never bothered Will before that he lived next door to a morgue, but that night he hardly slept at all knowing the story of the dead men that were currently laid out in there. When at last he did fall asleep, his dreams were filled with nightmares as he dreamt of those once happy looking men meeting their violent and drunken end.

Although Will's mother Caroline could neither read nor write herself, she knew the importance of an education. The older children were now bringing some money into the home; Will himself had managed to find work as an errand boy at a grocer's shop, which paid two shillings a week. With the money that the children were bringing in and with the money that she was making as a seamstress, she managed to find enough to send the children to school, which cost a penny a week for each of them. They went to George Green School on East India Dock Road; Will loved it. Caroline took great pride in her children's education.

One day as Will sat at home reading a magazine, his mother came into the room after being outside and told him that she had just invited one of the neighbours in so that Will could read to her. "Great!" was his response.

"Who is it this time?"

"Old mother Reynolds," she told him.

"Oh good! She always brings such great magazines and newspapers to read. I can't wait to see what she has this time." Caroline smiled at the pleasure that schooling obviously brought to Will. She knew he was a smart boy. Will went back to reading his book while they waited for their neighbour to arrive; a book that he had recently bought from the old man that came to all the houses in the area selling used books. Will was soon absorbed in it again and roared with laughter.

"What on earth is so funny?" his mother asked.

"This author is amazing!" Will told her. "His name is Charles Dickens. This book is called Oliver Twist and it's about a poor young lad who is sent to the workhouse just like me."

His mother frowned; the workhouse was no laughing matter to her, nor to Will usually, but he continued to tell her about the book anyway. "Oliver and the other boys in the workhouse are starving, so they draw lots to see who should ask for more food," he explains. "The task falls to Oliver, so he gets up from the dining table and asks for more food."

"I don't see anything funny about that!" she said, obviously not amused. But Will was still laughing and said, "Myself and everyone else in that wretched place have never felt hunger like it, but no one would ever dare to ask for more food. I can just picture the looks on those pompous officer's faces. I can't wait to read more by Dickens."

By now, Will had been working as an errand boy for three years. Although he was grateful for the work, he needed a job with better pay, so he set about finding other work.

One morning he set off down Commercial Road calling in at every shop and work place that he came across, seeking employment. He walked for hours without luck, nobody seemed to need such a small lad. At last he decided to turn around and make his way home. As he walked past Limehouse Causeway he heard the clang of metal on metal and noticed the open gates to a smithy's yard. He went to investigate. As he entered the smithy, one of the blacksmiths saw him. The smith, wearing a soot smeared collarless white shirt with his sleeves rolled up to his elbows beneath an open waistcoat asked, "What can we do for you lad?"

"I'm looking for work," Will told him.

"Can you blow the bellows, little un?" the smith asked, pointing to the large bellows that stood next to the forge.

"Yes, sir!" Will said excitedly. "I sure can!"

"All right then, lad," the smith said. "Give me an hour on the bellows and we'll see how you get on."

Will quickly removed his jacket while grinning from ear to ear and eagerly got to work on the bellows. After an hour the smith stopped him and said, "Lad, you're just what we want; you're hired. It'll be hard work mind. You'll need to start at six in the morning and work until eight at night, and sometimes we need to work overtime to finish a job, so that means sometimes we're here until 10 or even 12 o'clock midnight. Are you going to be able to manage that?"

"Yes, sir! That won't be a problem at all!"

"All right then, let's see you here tomorrow morning at six o'clock sharp."

Will, still grinning turned to leave. "Hey little un," the blacksmith called. Will stopped and looked back.

"What's your name?" the smith asked.

"Will, sir, Will Crooks."

"All right, Will, make sure you get a good night's sleep. You'll need it!"

At the end of his first day of work there, the smith said, "All right, Will lad, you can go home now." Will wiped the sweat away from his forehead with the back of his arm. His face was red from being so close to the forge all day. "Thank you, sir," he said. "Did I do all right today?"

"You did great, lad. We're very pleased with you."

Will beamed at this news. He had a proper job at last. He put on his jacket and walked over to where the coal was piled. He rubbed the coal with his hands and then rubbed his blackened hands onto his already sweaty face. The smith's stopped work and all looked on in bewilderment.

"Will, what on earth are you doing?" one of them asked.

As Will turned to walk out, he said, "I just want people to know I'm a working man now." The smith's all laughed, but that didn't stop Will from doing the same thing most nights before he left for home. He was proud to be a working man.

8

One morning in July, 1865, when Will was just 13 years old, he was working in the smithy, but it was unusually quiet as he tidied the workplace and swept the floor. There was only one smith in the smithy at the time and he said to Will, "You're quiet this morning, lad. What's on your mind?"

Will stopped sweeping and leant on his broom, "I was just thinking about the election; the Liberal candidate is on the hustings in Commercial Road this morning."

The smith laughed. "You're a bit young to be interested in politics aren't you lad?"

"It's never too young to be interested in the people that are running the country and making decisions in Parliament on your behalf," replied Will.

"On our behalf is it? When has a politician ever done anything for the likes of us? Mark my words young lad, politicians will promise you the world for your vote, but in the end, nothing ever changes for working men like us."

Will's face flushed, annoyed at the attitude of the smith, but also because he knew it was somewhat true, however, he wasn't going to give up hope. There must be some good politicians out there that deliver on the promises they make.

"Right then!" the smith said as he picked up his jacket and put it on. "I need to pop out for a short while to speak to a customer about his job. It's not that far so I won't be gone long. When I'm away, just keep yourself busy sweeping up and tidying everyone's work areas."

"Yes, sir!" said Will.

As soon as the smith left the smithy, Will poked his head out the door and watched him walk to the end of the street and disappear around the corner. He then quickly grabbed his own jacket and was already putting it on as he raced from the empty smithy towards Commercial Road and the hustings.

He didn't take any chances; he listened to the politician for long enough to satisfy his longing to hear the man talk and then rushed back to work, but when he turned a corner a few streets away from the smithy he froze when he saw the smith in front of him also walking back to work. He quickly ducked back around the corner out of sight and stood with his back against the wall desperately trying to think of what to do. He could feel his heart thumping in his chest. If he were caught skipping work he was sure they would give him the sack. What would he tell his mother? She would be so disappointed.

He knew of another way back to the smithy, but it was a much longer route and he doubted he would have enough time to get there before the smith, but there was no alternative and without another second's thought, he set off running as fast as he could. People stopped and stared as he sped past them as if being pursued by the devil himself.

When he reached Limehouse Causeway he felt like his lungs would burst. He peeked around the corner and his heart leapt when he saw that the smith wasn't even in sight yet, so he ran as fast as he could, pushed open the door of the smithy and dived headfirst inside. He'd made it, just. Flushed, sweating, and panting for breath he tried to get to his feet. As he lifted his head, his heart sank when he saw a large pair of black boots in front of him and then at the same time heard the booming voice of the boot's owner roar at him. "Where the hell have you been?"

Will's eyes widened in fear. In front of him stood the foreman who had turned up for work when Will was away to find the smithy unlocked and unattended. He was not happy.

"Only to see the state of the Poll, sir," Will stammered trying to stand upright.

"You'll see the state of the Poll on Saturday young lad," the foreman replied angrily.

"You're not giving me the sack are you?" Will asked nervously.

"Not this time, but if it happens again you'll be straight out the door, lad. I will be deducting a shilling from your wages though. Now back to work with you before I change my mind and do sack you."

"Yes, sir," said Will dejectedly. He was grateful not to be sacked, but a shilling was a lot for his family to be without and he knew his mother would be disappointed. He felt awful for letting her down and learned his lesson after being deducted the shilling from his wages. He never tried to skip work again.

As his time working at the smithy increased, so did his earnings and the family had enough money now to take an extra room upstairs in the house in the High Street.

On his way home from work one Saturday afternoon, he stopped by an old book stall and looked through the books on sale. He picked up a copy of Homer's 'The Iliad'. "Now there's a classic," said the stall holder. "If it's excitement you want and tales of adventure in far away lands, that's the book to read. It's been thrilling its readers for thousands of years that one."
Will scoffed thinking the book seller was exaggerating. "Thousands of years?" he said disbelievingly.

"Yes my lad. That story was written by Homer, an ancient Greek poet thousands of years ago. It's all about the Trojan War."

"How much is it?" Will asked.

"Tuppence to you lad and I'm so sure you'll love it that if you don't, just bring it back and I'll give you your money back."

Will grinned. "I'll take it then," he said.

Not even the glowing report that the book seller had given him prepared Will's young mind for the wonders of Homer. He had never read anything like it before. Will read with wide eyed wonder the colourful tale of the Trojan war and of Helen of Troy, the face that launched a thousand ships. After a long day at work, he raced home so that he could be transported from the dreary East End to that far away world full of Greek gods and heroes. He thought his heart would burst from the suspense and excitement. He was so thankful that his mother had been able to send him to school.

Winter, 1866

Will's love of reading was well known to his workmates, especially his love of Shakespeare and his plays. One evening just before he finished work for the day and was about to head for home, one of the smiths shouted "Oi Will, give us a bit of Shakespeare before you go, lad."

As ever, Will was happy to oblige. He looked around the work place and found a ball of string that he picked up and pretended was a skull. As theatrically as he could, he launched into a scene from Hamlet; the glow from the forge acting as his stage lights.

"Alas, poor Yorick! I knew him well, Horatio; a fellow of infinite jest, of most excellent fancy; he hath borne me on his back a thousand times; and now, how abhorred in my imagination it is!" and in that manner he continued until the end of the scene.

When he finished his performance, his grime covered workmates as always applauded enthusiastically as if they were actually at the theater watching the play. Will of course did a low bow to the further delight of his workmates. He knew how to work the crowd. He ran home happily in the cold knowing that tomorrow was Sunday, his day off.

The next day as he relaxed at home reading, this time a Penny Dreadful story of Dick Turpin, the legendary Highwayman, he was disturbed by a great roar of raised voices and a commotion coming from outside.

"Whatever is that?" his mother asked.

Will jumped up and together they went to investigate. When they opened the street door they could see that all hell was breaking loose in front of the workhouse gates. 1866 had been a bad trade year for the workers of Poplar, which meant that every day a long line of hundreds of hungry men formed at the gates of the workhouse waiting to be handed a 2 lb. loaf of bread. Today, the cold, hungry and desperate men just couldn't wait; they were attacking the bread wagon before it could even get into the workhouse yard and a full blown riot was taking place with men fighting against each other to get some bread to take home to their families. It was a harrowing sight; one that Will would never forget. As he and his mother looked on in horror, the 14 year old boy vowed, "When I grow up to be a man, I'm going to do all that I can to help these poor unfortunate people."

9

At the end of his third year at the smithy, Will was earning six shillings a week. As small as this amount was, it helped out enormously at home, but Will felt that he had spent long enough being a bellows boy. One morning while at work during a quiet period, Will asked the foreman if he could have a talk with him. "Of course, Will lad, what can I do for you?" the foreman asked.

"Well sir, I've been in the job as the bellows boy for three years now and I was wondering if you had plans for me to learn the trade? You've seen what a hard worker I am and I learn very quickly." The foreman laid a hand on Will's shoulder. "I know you are, Will. We can't fault you on your work rate and that's a fact, but to be honest lad, we don't have any plans for you to learn the trade from us. I'm sorry."

Will's heart sank. It wasn't the answer that he had been expecting. He bit down on his lower lip to stop it from quivering and blinked back tears. He managed an accepting nod of his head and stepped back out of the reach of the foreman so the man was forced to remove his hand from Will's shoulder. Will was too upset to speak, so he went about his work with his head lowered to avoid any contact with his fellow workmen. He had never been promised that he would be taught the trade, but after being there for so long he had thought that would just be the obvious progression. He felt hurt and betrayed. When he got home that night he ate in silence with a heavy heart. "What on earth is wrong with you tonight, Will? You're unusually quiet," his mother said with concern.

"I asked the foreman today if I was going to learn the trade and he said, no, that they had no plans to train me as a smith and that I'm to remain a labourer there."

"What?" she cried, clearly annoyed. "After you've put in three years of hard work there! They have some nerve! Well I'm not having you work there any longer, do you hear me? Tell them you'll work until the end of the week if they need you to, but once you get paid, that's it."

"But how will we cope without my money coming in?" he asked.

"We'll cope," she said. "Next week we'll start looking for an apprenticeship for you. We'll just have to make sacrifices until we get you fixed up somewhere where you'll have a trade under your belt and a future."

Will was sad to leave the smithy and his friends after having been there for so long, but he knew his mother was right. He needed and wanted a trade. He didn't have to wait long for one either. With her usual determination, Caroline was quickly able to find Will an apprenticeship at a Coopers yard. It only paid two shillings a week, which was four shillings less than what he was earning at the smiths, but she was willing to sacrifice the money coming in now for the benefit of Will's long term future. When Will turned up for his first morning of work at the Coopers yard, he couldn't have been happier. There were five other apprentices there that were roughly his own age. After being the only boy at the smithy for so long, it felt great to be able to work with boys his own age. Every day at work was fun, but even so, he still took his apprenticeship seriously and worked hard.

Will had been at the Coopers for about six months when one day as he sat eating his packed lunch with the other apprentices, one of them, Sam, said, "I wish the company would pay us apprentices more. I could really do with more money to help out at home. For the long hours that we work, the company should also pay us more for overtime too. I love the job don't get me wrong, but we seem to be here all the time." Another apprentice, Joe, spoke up, "I agree, I don't know how I would manage without my Sunday job."

Will looked surprised, "What Sunday job?" he asked.

Sam laughed, "Why didn't you know, Will? Joe's old man is an undertaker. On Sundays when there's a funeral, Joe walks in front of the funeral procession as the mute." Will looked confused. "You're joking, right?" he asked.

"Not at all," Sam laughed. "Come on, Joe," he said to the other boy, "show us how it's done."

"Yeah, come on Joe," the other boys cried, trying to egg him on.

Joe rolled his eyes like he didn't want to do it, but his body language suggested otherwise and he jumped to his feet. Joe was the tallest of the apprentices; he was also thin with a mop of black hair. "Right then," he said, "now you have to imagine though that I'm wearing my black suit and black top hat and behind me is the funeral procession with the horses pulling the hearse."

"One minute, Joe," Sam said as he grabbed a bucket and placed it on Joe's head to make do as a top hat. He then went and fetched a small wheelbarrow. "Oi Fred!" he called to another of the apprentices. "You're small, get in here and pretend you're dead." Fred was a small, thin boy with a dirty face and short cropped blond hair. He laughed and jumped into the wheelbarrow, his small framed torso fitting easily inside as his short legs hung dangling out over the front. He then lay down, closed his eyes and crossed his arms across his chest, thus resembling a smiling corpse.

Joe then put on his best solemn Sunday face as he led the funeral procession through the coopery, while the other boys fell about laughing.

"Oi! Have a bit of bleedin' respect for the dead will you before you all get a clip around the ear," shouted one of the coopers, clearly annoyed. The procession came to an abrupt halt. The boys then sat giggling out of earshot of the angry cooper while they finished their lunch. When they had settled down, Will asked, "Do you really get paid for just walking in front of a funeral procession?"

"Yeah," said Joe, "but it's not much. Do you think we should go and ask the boss for more money?" he asked. Some of the other boys looked scared.

"If we do," said Sam, "all of us should go together."

"Hands up all that's in favour of going then?" asked Joe.

One by one they all nervously raised their hands.

"When shall we do it then?" asked Will.

"Well there's no time like the present," Sam said decisively.

"Who's going to do the talking?" asked Fred.

Sam looked at Joe. "Well, Joe's the oldest," he said. Joe took a deep breath and then blew out his cheeks. He gave a quick nod. "All right!" he said. "I can do it, but what do I say?"

"We'll help you memorise a speech; you'll be fine." Will assured him.

Before their break for lunch was over, Joe was as ready as he would ever be. He looked extremely nervous. The boss's office was upstairs and it overlooked the main workshop. They climbed the dark green industrial looking metal staircase in silence and then made their way along the metal walkway that led to the boss's office. On their left was a handrail, which stopped people falling off the walkway into the work area below and to their right was a large window that the boss could look out of to keep an eye on what was going on below without leaving his office. As the boys made their way across the walkway in front of the window, they caught their boss's eye and he looked up from his desk and watched them file past. All five boys then stood in front of the office door looking and feeling very nervous; some of them were actually shaking. Joe, being the spokesperson stood at the front of the small group. Even though he was the tallest and the eldest amongst them, he couldn't help but shake nervously too. Just as Joe was about to knock on the boss's office door, Will whispered, "Joe, put on your best Sunday face." Everyone laughed and the tension was broken, but unfortunately so was their resolve. All the boys apart from Will fell over each other as they panicked in their haste to flee from the office. As they did so, the boss, upon seeing the boys approach through his window opened his office door to see what was going on. Only Will was left standing there. After the boss watched the last of the boys

Where there's a Will, there's a way

disappear at the end of the walkway and fly down the stairs, he looked down at Will.

"What's this about, Crooks?" he asked.

"It's about our pay and conditions, sir," said Will, confidently.

"Is it now," said the boss. "and what's wrong with your pay and conditions?"

"Well, sir," Will began, "although we all love the job, we feel that our current pay doesn't reflect the hard work that we do, and with all the overtime that we're asked to work we hardly have any time to spend with our families, sir." The boss looked thoughtful for a while and then said, "Those are pretty serious issues that you've raised, Crooks; so tell me, why did the other lads run away laughing?"

"Well, sir, on Sundays, Joe helps his father who is a funeral director. He walks in front of the funeral procession as a mute. He was supposed to be our spokesman, but just before you opened the door I whispered that he should put on his best Sunday face to greet you." The boss roared with laughter. When he finished laughing, he said. "Right then, let's get back to work, Crooks. I know you're all a bunch of hard workers. You can tell your friends that I'm raising all your pay and cutting the amount of overtime you'll have to work."

"Thank you, sir," Will grinned. "I'll tell them and I know they'll be as grateful as I am."

A week after their improved conditions took effect, Sam turned up for work an hour late. The next day, an hour after start time had passed and he still hadn't arrived.

"I don't know," said the foreman shaking his head. "The guvnor gives you lads a pay increase and cuts the amount of overtime you have to work and this is the way you repay him." Although it was unfair of the foreman to berate all of them for Sam being late, they did agree with him that it was not the way to repay their boss and they all felt badly.

"Can we borrow the wheelbarrow for a few minutes?" Joe asked the foreman.

"What for?" he wanted to know.

"Two of us will go round to Sam's house, wake him up and dump him in the wheelbarrow. The embarrassment of being pushed through the streets like that should help wake him up in the mornings." The foreman laughed and gave his blessings. Joe and Will took the wheelbarrow and pushed it to Sam's house and banged on his front door.

"Right then, Will," Joe whispered, "as soon as Sam comes to the door, let's grab him and throw him into the wheelbarrow."

Out of the corner of his eye, Will saw a slight movement from the curtains in the nearby window.

"I just saw the curtains move," Will whispered to Joe. "He may have seen us." Joe went to the window and looked into the house. He just managed to spot Sam pulling up his trousers, with his jacket under his arm disappearing out the back door. "He's away out the back door!" Joe cried.

Meanwhile at the back of the house, Sam leapt over the garden wall into the house next door's backyard and landed in a flower bed. A woman came running out of the house waving her fist at him, "You little bugger!" she screamed as Sam quickly clambered up and over the next garden wall only to land on top of a dog that was just rousing from a nap after being woken by the woman cursing next door. The startled dog yelped, but quickly sprung to life and tore aggressively at Sam's trousers. Sam tried desperately to clamber over the next wall while trying to keep the dog at bay by lashing out with his feet and he finally managed to escape its gnashing jaws and dropped over the wall and landed with a thud on cobbles below.

He allowed himself a few seconds to recover as he gingerly got to his feet, while the dog continued to bark angrily. He had landed in a narrow access alley that ran between the houses on either side of it. The alley led to the street. He ran through it as fast as his badly torn trousers would allow, but the noise from the dog had already alerted Joe and Will to what he was up to. As soon as he stepped foot onto the street from the alley, Joe and Will were after him like a shot and they almost ran him over with the wheelbarrow. "Oi, careful!" he screamed at his friends as he took off as fast as he could with Joe and Will snapping at his heels with the wheelbarrow.

The workmen in the Coopery, along with the other apprentices jumped in alarm when the doors came crashing open and Sam collapsed in a panting heap onto the sawdust covered floor, with one trouser leg torn to shreds. Joe and Will then came crashing in behind him and everyone including the foreman laughed at the mess that was Sam sprawled all over the floor. He was never late again.

Some months later, the boys all gathered together as they usually did when they stopped to eat lunch, but today, Will did not join them. Instead, he found a quiet corner and sat down to read. "Hey Will, aren't you joining us?" called Joe.

"Not today, Joe," Will replied. "I love this book I'm reading and I want to read as much of it as I can."

"What is it?" Joe asked. "One of those Dickens books you're always talking about?"

"No, it's called Alton Locke." Will told him.

"Hey Joe," Sam called. "Come and join us and leave Will alone if he doesn't want to join us."

"Have fun then," Joe said as he went to join the other boys.

A few minutes later, Will heard somebody approach. It was one of the coopers named Charlie.

"Hello Will," he said quietly. Charlie was a reserved man and he usually kept himself to himself. When Will glanced up he looked annoyed, but not at being disturbed by Charlie; he was just annoyed at what he had read. Charlie noticed the look and smiled, "I can see why a lad like you would get stirred up by a book like Alton Locke."

"You've read it?" Will asked in amazement. Not many people he came into contact with liked to read books, especially books like Alton Locke.

"Can I sit down with you?" Charlie asked.

"Of course," said Will.

"Oh yes, Will, I've read Alton Locke all right, and the more people that do read books like that the better our lot as the working class will become. I've heard some of the things you've been saying around here, Will, about reform and better conditions for the poor and the working classes as a whole and I like what I hear. I share a lot of your ideas and thoughts, but I have a family to provide for so I keep my views mostly to myself. Getting myself a reputation as a radical or an agitator is something I just can't afford to do. I'd be grateful if you said nothing of the nature of our chat to anyone else."

"Not a word!" Will assured him, looking around for any signs of eavesdroppers.

"I can tell by the look on your face when you're reading Alton Locke that it's tugging away at something inside of you," Charlie said.

"It's just the unjustness of the working class's lot," whispered Will. "I know this book is opening people's eyes to the unjustness of it all, but it's painful to read when you live amongst it. I like the way Charles Kingsley is showing that we need more social and political reforms that will benefit the working classes. He's saying there must be room for fairness and compassion."

"He is indeed," Charlie said smiling, obviously impressed by Will's awareness.

"Do you know much about John Bright?" asked Charlie.

"No, not much," said Will.

"Well, John Bright is a radical MP from up north, and quite the reformer. He's also a considerable public speaker. The way he gets his message across is by the power and emotion of his speeches. His speeches often attack the privileges of the landed aristocracy and he said that their selfishness regarding the setting of prices under the Corn Law, which kept food prices artificially high was causing the working classes a great deal of suffering. He argued against this Corn Law and called on the working classes and the middle classes to unite and fight for free trade and cheaper food. I have some papers of his at home I could let you read if you like; there are a lot of his speeches in there too."

"Yes please!" said Will, enthusiastically. "I'd love that!"

"But not a word that they came from me. Is that clear?" Charlie whispered.

"I promise! Not a word to anyone!" Will assured him.

"Right then," said Charlie. "I'd better get back to work. I'll bring those papers in tomorrow."

A few weeks later when Charlie was at his workbench alone, Will took the opportunity to approach him. "I've finished reading all about John Bright," he whispered. Charlie quickly glanced around to make sure that nobody was in earshot.

"What did you think?" he asked.

"I was very impressed by the man, especially his passion, his convictions and most of all by his speeches," said Will. He then quoted, "The angel of Death has been abroad throughout the land. You may almost hear the beating of his wings."

"Powerful stuff," said Charlie. "He certainly has a way with words that one." Will nodded and said somewhat in awe.

"Powerful stuff indeed! His speeches stir the imagination in a way that you can't help but hear his point. Do you have anything else that I can read?" Will asked.

"Tomorrow I'll bring in something about Richard Cobden," Charlie said. "He was also a campaigner against the Corn Law, and was actually the man who enlisted John Bright to the cause."

"Great!" said Will, smiling enthusiastically. "I can't wait!"

When Will had finished reading about Richard Cobden, Charlie brought in some magazines for him to read.

"What are these?" Will asked.

"They're called 'The British Workman'. You'll enjoy reading these, Will. They're trying to educate and improve the lot of the British workman, but at the same time they are fun to read and poke fun at the ruling classes. I've more where that came from when you've finished." Charlie was right, Will loved reading them and they soon became one of Will's favorite reading materials.

10

A Few Years Later

One morning, Will stepped out of the cooper's workshop into the yard carrying some off-cuts of wood and threw them on top of a pile in a corner. Just inside the entrance of the yard, sitting on a low wall was a young girl of Will's age. He walked over to where she sat and smiling broadly said, "Hello, you're Mr. South the shipwright's daughter aren't you?"

"Yes, that's right," the girl answered, curious to know how he knew who she was. "How do you know that?" she asked.

"Oh, I've seen you here a few times now," said Will. "Is your father inside?" he asked.

"Yes," said the girl. "I hate going in there. It's so stuffy."

"You want to see it away from the offices down in the workshop. Down there it's stuffy 'and' hot."

"What's your work?" she asked him.

"I'm an apprenticed cooper," Will announced proudly.

"Good!" she said smiling. She obviously approved.

"You know what my father does," she said. "What does your father do?" Will hung his head a little and said sadly, "Oh, he died last year."

"Oh, I'm sorry," the girl said sympathetically.

"He lost an arm in an accident when I was no more than a baby so finding any type of work was difficult for him," Will told her. "My name's, Will, by the way," he said, changing the subject. "What's yours?"

"Tilly!" she answered. "Short for Matilda."

"Ah Tilly," said Will as he took off his cap and playfully held it in both hands over his heart.

"That which we call a rose by any other name would smell as sweet." Tilly giggled and said, "Well bless my soul, that's the first time I've ever had Shakespeare quoted at me."

"You knew it was Shakespeare?" Will asked, pleasantly surprised.

"I've read quite a bit of Shakespeare," she told him.

"Me too," laughed Will. "So you like to read then?" he added.

"I'm never happier than when I have a book with me," she said.

"Me too!" Will blurted out, almost shouting.

"Oi! Will!" came the shout from the foreman who was standing at the open workshop door. "There's work in here to be done, lad."

"As you can see I've got to go," sighed Will. "Once more into the breach dear friends," he quoted theatrically from Henry V as he hurried away.

Tilly laughed as she waved goodbye. Will could barely concentrate on his work for the rest of the day and more than once did a colleague ask what the big soppy grin on his face was for.

As the days and weeks passed, Will made a habit of peeking through the open doors that led to the yard to see if he could spot Tilly again. At last the day came when she reappeared. This time she wasn't sitting on the wall, but was pacing back and forth in front of it, glancing across the yard every now and then at the doors where Will had disappeared through the last time she was there. Will was well prepared for this moment and he pretended to trip over some loose wood off-cuts. "Just going to take these off-cuts to the yard, Guv," he announced. Tilly wore a long navy blue dress which was finished with a cream coloured sash around her narrow waist and a bow tied at her back. Her crinoline petticoat gave the outfit its bell shape. Beneath her small cream bonnet, the fringe of her long brown hair covered her forehead and beneath the fringe her two pretty hazel eyes lit up when she saw Will. Once outside, he dumped the wood as quickly as he could and walked over to where she stood.

"Hello again," he said.

"Hello, Will," she said, smiling shyly.

"You remembered my name," he said happily.

"Of course!" she said.

Will thought she looked beautiful. In total contrast he looked a mess in his tattered work apron that only partly covered some of his old work shirt that he wore with his sleeves rolled up above his elbows. It may have bothered some people, but Will was proud to be a working man, and working men often looked dirty because of their jobs. The important thing was that Tilly didn't seem to have a problem with the way he looked.

"Have you read any good books recently?" Will asked.

"As a matter of fact I have," she replied eagerly. "I've just read 'The old curiosity shop' by Charles Dickens."

"I love that book!" cried Will excitedly. "In fact I've read nearly everything by Dickens."

"He's a favourite of mine too," she said, smiling. "I just love 'Great Expectations'. Miss Havisham is so strange isn't she? I've never read anything like it before. The man is a genius."

"But why Pip would love Estella so much and then want to marry her is beyond me," said Will, looking confused.

"Boys," sighed Tilly, rolling her eyes and shaking her head playfully.

"What?" said Will, looking even more confused. "She was horrible to him."

Where there's a Will, there's a way

"Ah, but as our mutual friend Shakespeare says, 'Love is blind.'" Tilly sighed theatrically. Will felt awkward now talking about love to Tilly. He didn't know what to say next, so he looked around back at the workshop door hoping that the foreman would be there about to call him back to work again, but he wasn't. Will nodded back towards the door anyway.

"I really should be getting back before my foreman comes looking for me again," he said. "Do you know when you'll be back here again?"

"No," she sighed. "Soon I hope."

"I hope so too," said Will.

A few days later, Will looked up from his work and saw his foreman talking to Mr. South at the bottom of the stairs that led up to the offices. They glanced over in Will's direction. He felt his face redden. They were obviously talking about him. Did Mr. South find out that he had been talking to his daughter? Was he here to protect her reputation? So many questions raced around inside his head. The foreman walked over to Will. "Mr. South, the shipwright would like a word with you, Will." He tried to remain calm, but inside is heart was pounding. He put down his tools and noticed that he was shaking. He then wiped his hands on his apron and walked over to where Mr. South stood waiting for him. "So you're Will are you?" Mr. South asked, carefully eyeing him up and down.

"Yes, sir." Will answered nervously.

"Tilly tells me that you share her love of books," he said.

"Oh yes, sir!" Will said with relief while managing a slight smile. "I try to read whenever I get a spare moment."

"Where did you learn to read?" Mr. South asked.

"At Sunday school and George Green school, sir," Will answered.

"Good," said Mr. South nodding approvingly. "Your foreman tells me that you're a skillful and hardworking lad. Do you like your trade?"

"Yes sir, I do," answered Will, beginning to relax now. "I take great pride in everything I make."

"Good for you lad!" said Mr. South. "May I ask where you live, Will?" he added.

"Down on the High Street, sir," Will told him. Mr. South handed Will a piece of paper that had an address written on it. "Do you know where this is lad?"

"Yes, sir," nodded Will.

"Can you be there at 3 o'clock on Sunday afternoon for tea?" Will's jaw nearly struck the ground. Mr. South laughed when he saw the look of surprise on Will's face. "It'll be nothing fancy," he warned. "But it's rare indeed to find someone of Tilly's age who shares her love of books."

"Thank you," Will said, still a little stunned. "I'd love to come."

11

Two years later, and after many more Sunday afternoon tea times, Tilly almost ran to the door when she heard the knocking. As expected, Will stood on the doorstep in his Sunday finest. He smiled and doffed his cap. "Come on in," she told him excitedly and then called, "Father! Will is here!"

"I'm in the back room," her father called back. "Come on in."

Will followed Tilly into the room, which was covered in a wallpaper that was decorated in wide columns of dark and light green. A large oil painting of a Tea Clipper fighting its way through rough seas hung above the cluttered mantelpiece, and a small desk made of Walnut stood in front of the open, dark green curtains, allowing sunlight to stream into the room. As Will and Tilly entered, Mr. South was just getting up out of his chair by the desk.

"Hello, sir," Will said nervously as he held out his hand for Mr. South to shake. Tilly's father took his hand and shook it firmly. "Tilly tells me you have something you want to talk to me about."

"Yes, sir," Will replied, his hands nervously playing with his cap in his hands. He cleared his throat, "Well I'm 19 now and I've finished my apprenticeship, which means I'm getting a full working man's wage now and with your permission I'd like to ask Tilly to be my wife."

Mr. South's face was expressionless as he looked across at his daughter who blushed, but held his gaze. "And how do you feel about this, Tilly?" he asked. "Is this something that you would agree to?"

"Oh yes, Father!" she said excitedly.

He held out both hands towards her and smiled, so she stepped forward and placed her hands in his. He looked her up and down like it was the first time he had truly seen her. "Oh my, Tilly, you've grown so fast. Where did the time go? How can you be a woman already?" Then his smile disappeared for a few seconds as a fleeting look of sadness crossed his face as he realised his little girl was no longer a child, but a young woman. When he turned back to Will, however, his smile returned and still holding Tilly's hands he said, "Not only do I give my permission, but I give you my blessing too. I hope you'll both be very happy together."

"Oh thank you!" Tilly cried as she threw her arms around her father's neck and hugged him tightly.

When she let him go, Will was waiting to shake Mr. South's hand. "Thank you, sir," Will said. "I'll take good care of her."

Mr. South shook Will's hand. "I know you will, lad. Now Tilly, let me go and break the news to your mother."

Where there's a Will, there's a way

As soon as her father left the room, Tilly threw her arms around Will's neck this time and together they hugged.

The morning of the wedding in December 1871 was overcast and cold, but as Will and Tilly left St. Thomas's church in Bethnal Green, East London, neither of them noticed. Their friends and family cheered them on as they climbed into the carriage that took them to their new home, which comprised of two rooms that Will had found them near his work at the Coopery. It was a happy time for Will. Here he was, a working man with a trade that he was proud of, and waiting for him at home was a lovely, smart, young wife. Tilly soon became pregnant and they decided to move to a small house in time for the birth of their first child; a daughter who they named Matilda Faith.

At work, however, things began to change. Will took great pride in his work and had always been happy at the Coopery, but when the management changed, they took to bringing in a poorer quality of wood to use with the aim of saving money and boosting profits. Will was not impressed. Then the news came that overtime was to be increased. The men were not happy. The need for workers' rights and his pride in the quality of his workmanship brought matters to a head. Even though he was one of the youngest men there, he called his fellow workers together.

When he was sure there was no management around, he said to his colleagues, "Look everyone, I've heard you all complaining about all this new overtime that we are being made to do. I for one have a young family that I want to spend time with. I know most of you do too. I love my work, but I don't want to spend all my life here. And what is this cheap and nasty wood business all about? How are we to put our best efforts into making something that we as craftsmen should be proud of, when we are forced to use such substandard materials. It will come to no good, you mark my words. What will our customers do when they find that the barrels that we send them don't last half as long as they did before because of the poor quality of the wood that we are now using? Where will their custom go then? To us still? I doubt it very much, and where will our jobs be then? This is a time for us to stand up for our rights as workers. We need to approach the management over this and let them know our views and get things changed before they get any worse. Now who's with me?" he asked.

A few of the men said, "I am Will," but in the main the men were unsure as to what to do.

"Give us a few days to think on it, Will," said one.

"Good idea," agreed the others.

"All right then," a disappointed Will agreed. "Take a few days to think it over, but mark my words, we need to take action on this before it's too late."

The next day when Will arrived at work, he started to take his jacket off and hang it on the hook above his work area as he did every morning, when the foreman came over.

"You don't need to take your jacket off today, Will," the foreman said sadly.

"Why? What's wrong?" asked Will, confused.

The foreman stepped closer and handed Will some money.

"What's this?" asked Will.

The foreman looked uncomfortable, "I'm sorry, Will, but that's your wages. I've got to let you go."

"What?" gasped Will. "Why?"

The foreman nodded back towards where the offices were. "The management got wind of your little speech yesterday," he said. "They don't want an agitator among the men."

Will rummaged in his jacket pocket and then pulled out his trade union card. He waved it defiantly in front of the foreman. "One day all workers will hold one of these and then we'll have some rights. You mark my words!" He gathered up his belongings and left.

Tilly was alarmed when she heard somebody entering the house so early in the day. "Is that you, Will?" she called from the sitting room where she was sat feeding the baby.

"Hello love," he said in a voice that was both sad and angry as he entered the room.

"Will, what on earth is the matter?" she asked, looking distressed.

"They let me go because of my talk with the men yesterday. Management got wind of it and told me to leave because they said I'm an agitator."

"Oh Will, I'm sorry, but what are we going to do for money?" she asked.

"Don't worry, I have my trade. I'll get something soon enough," he assured her.

Tilly stood up, still cradling the baby and went to Will and kissed him. "I'm proud of you, Will, for standing up for yourself," she said in support.

"Thanks love," he said. "That means a lot to me. I'll go out soon and look for work. I know of a few places where I should be able to find work easily enough."

12

At the first workshop that Will visited in his search for work, he walked inside where he saw one of the workmen leaning over some wood and making marks on it with a thick pencil. "Can I speak to the foreman?" Will asked.

"I'm the foreman!" the man said as he straightened up and placed the pencil behind his right ear. "What can I do for you?" asked the stocky, moustached man as he approached Will.

"I'm looking for work," said Will. "I'm a cooper by trade."

"Are you now?" said the foreman suspiciously. "What's your name?"

"Will Crooks," said Will.

The foreman shook his head, "We don't need anyone," he said coldly.

The next place Will tried he got the same reply, and again at the place after that, and from the place after that too. He spent the rest of the day walking the streets of Poplar visiting places where he thought he would easily be able to find work, but at each place he was told the same news; they didn't need anyone.

The next day, Will set out early to try further afield. He walked to Rotherhithe. He knew of a few places there where he was fairly certain he could find work. At the first workshop he visited that day he knocked on the door and when it was opened asked to see the foreman. "I'm the foreman here. How can I help you?" asked the smiling man that had opened the door.

"I'm looking for work," said Will. "I'm a cooper by trade."

"What's your name?" the foreman asked, his smile quickly fading.

"Crooks," answered Will.

"Of Poplar?" asked the foreman.

"That's me," said Will.

"We don't need anyone," the foreman said as he closed the door on Will. Will's heart sank. Word had obviously spread quickly that he was viewed as an agitator. Everywhere else he tried in Rotherhithe he was met with the same response.

On the days and weeks that followed, he walked to Hackney, Clerkenwell, Battersea and then most of London, but word had spread everywhere in the Capital that Will Crooks the Cooper was an agitator. It was becoming obvious that Will was not going to be able to find work in London, and the lack of money was beginning to be felt at home.

He decided to head down to the docks to see if he could find work there. He knew of the two or three times a day call-on and knew the pay wasn't good, but he needed work. When he arrived at the dock gates he was shocked by the amount of men already gathered there waiting for the foreman to call on the lucky men that he favoured for a few hours work that day. When the foreman appeared, the waiting men lunged forward pushing others out of their way as they scrambled to get to the front of the crowd. Will saw men fall and then get trampled as the crowd relentlessly pushed forward. He also watched as men came to blows as they fought to get into view of the foreman. Will felt sick to his stomach as he witnessed the crowd's desperation and in a daze he found himself being pushed forward by the surge of men behind him. He desperately tried to stay on his feet and without quite knowing how, he soon found himself near the front of the crowd.

"Will!" he heard somebody shout above the noise of the crowd. He looked up to see that the foreman was somebody that he knew from his days at the smithy.

"Will!" he called again and waved him forward. As desperate for work as he was, Will knew that he couldn't take work away from any of these poor fellows around him. He had a trade. He knew he would find work eventually, but not like this, not by taking work away from men that were less fortunate than him. This is all these men had. Will turned his back on the foreman and pushed his way out through the crowd as quickly as he could.

Will realised that if he wanted work, he would have to leave London to find it. He and Tilly made the decision that Will would look for work further afield while Tilly took the baby and stayed with her parents until Will could find work and send for them. Armed only with his trade union card that would enable him to claim half a crown at those towns where the union had branches, he set out on his quest for work. From town to town he tramped all day asking for work, none was found.

As he walked towards the town of Burton upon Trent, he had already walked over 100 miles since he left London and the soles of his shoes finally gave out; he could walk in them no more; his feet were blistered and painful. He sat down by the side of the road and tried to fight back his despair and tears. He was hungry, footsore and exhausted. All he could do was sit and hold his head in his hands.

"Are you all right, friend?" a shaky old voice asked.
Will looked up at the concerned face of an old tramp.

"No, not really," said Will. "I've been on the road for weeks looking for work with no luck and now the soles of my shoes have given out and my feet are so sore that I don't think I can walk any further."

"Let's see your shoes," the tramp said to Will. "I may be able to help there."

Will took off one of his shoes and showed it to the tramp. "I can fix that for you," he said. "It won't look pretty, but you'll be able to walk in them for a while longer." The tramp put down the large bag that he was carrying that held his worldly possessions and began rummaging inside it. "Ah, here we go," he said and pulled out a couple of pieces of string.

"When was the last time you ate?" he asked Will.

"Yesterday evening," replied Will.

"You hungry?" the tramp asked.

Will could only nod yes as his stomach growled at the thought of food.

"I don't have much myself," the tramp said, "but I have a little bread that I can share if you don't mind where it came from."

Will hated the thought of taking food from this man who needed it so badly himself, but he was so weak and hungry that he accepted the offer. He made a point of not asking where it came from and he was glad the tramp didn't offer up that information. While Will ate his bread, the tramp got to work on the shoes. He turned the shoes upside down, got Will to put his feet on the uppers and then tied them to Will's feet. When he had finished, he helped Will to his feet and got him to walk around in them. They were far from comfortable, but at least he would be able to walk again.

"Are you about to enter Burton, or are you leaving it?" the tramp asked.

"I'm just about to enter it," said Will.

"Good," said the tramp, grinning through rotten teeth. "That's where I'm headed. Would you like some company?"

"That sounds just great," said Will.

Burton upon Trent was just like the other towns that he had visited, nothing was available to him, but just as he was about to give up all hope, one of the foremen that he spoke to said, "We don't have much going on at the moment, but I know a couple of local men that moved to Liverpool and found work as soon as they arrived there, but if you don't have transport then it's going to be about an 80 mile walk for you."

"Thank you," Will said gratefully. "It may be a long walk, but at least I have some glimmer of hope again to get me there."

When he reached Liverpool he could barely walk and was near to exhaustion, however, just like the men the friendly foreman had known, he found work almost at once. He was hired as a cooper in the brewery of Robert Cain and Sons. He then found a bed at the YMCA (The Young Men's Christian Association had been formed 28 years earlier in 1844 in London) and collapsed into it and slept for the rest of that day and through the night.

At the end of his first week, the foreman went around to all of the men and handed them their pay. Will couldn't help but grin from ear to ear. He had never been so happy to see a wage packet.

"You look happy to see that," laughed the foreman.

"Oh I am," said Will as he took his wages and kissed them. "The first thing I'm going to do with this is send my wife in London money for the train fare to Liverpool so that she and our baby daughter can join me here."

Will arrived at the railway station early to meet the train. He paced up and down the platform waiting impatiently for his young family to arrive. The smell of the smoke from the other steam trains hung in the air and at last he heard the whistle from the train from London announcing its arrival into the station. When he saw Tilly getting out of the carriage carrying the baby he almost broke down. He had missed them so much. He ran and threw his arms around them, "What a sight for sore eyes you two are to me, Tilly. It makes all that I've endured recently worthwhile now that we're all together again." He then turned his attention to his baby daughter who was crying loudly in Tilly's arms. "There now little one, what's all the crying for? Aren't you happy to see your father again?"

"She's been fussing all the way up here on the train," said Tilly. "I don't know what's wrong with her."

"Come along then," he said, concerned. "I'll take you to the room that I've found for us. Let's get her home and out of this smoky air."

The next day, Will almost ran home after work in his eagerness to see his wife and child, however, when he arrived home he found that the baby had still not settled. He picked her up and cradled her in his arms, "There, there, young miss," he soothed. "What's the matter? You should be happy now that we're all together again."

"I think it's just the train journey making her a bit poorly," said Tilly. "All that smoke in the air couldn't have done her much good. I wish my mother was here to take a look."

"I'm afraid I'm not earning enough to send her the fare just yet," said Will.

"Nor would she come all this way," sighed Tilly. She gently stroked Matilda's pale cheek. "I'm sure she'll pick up when she settles in properly."

"I hope so," said Will.

By the end of the week the poor little baby was no better and just wouldn't settle. After another long day at work, Will returned home and after checking on his daughter, he and Tilly sat and quietly chatted. He had missed her so much when he had left her in London. Tilly, being the one used to Matilda's crying throughout the day was the first to notice the silence. She looked across the room at the baby. "This is the quietest she's been since we arrived," she said.

"Hopefully she'll get some much needed sleep," said Will.

"We all will," said Tilly, gratefully.

Will looked lovingly at Tilly. She looked exhausted. She then closed her eyes and took a well-earned nap. Will looked at them both sleeping, and after the long and tiring day that he had just had, he also closed his eyes to nap.

He awoke when he heard Tilly getting up from her chair and watched as she crossed the room to check on the baby. She stood and smiled as she looked down at her little daughter sleeping peacefully. However, Will noticed her smile quickly disappear when she couldn't see any signs of breathing from the baby. "Will!" she called anxiously as she bent over to check the baby.

Will leapt up from his chair and rushed to her side. She had her ear to Matilda's chest. "Will!" she wailed, "I think she's dead!" As she straightened up and threw her hands over her mouth in horror, she stared wide eyed as Will quickly leant over and picked up his child. She was cold and lifeless.

Later the next morning, Will entered the room; he had been out arranging the burial. Tilly was lying face down on the bed, her face hidden in the crook of her arm, she was still crying inconsolably.

"We can bury her tomorrow," Will said sadly. Tilly just continued to sob.

"Have you eaten anything?" he asked.

"No," she sniffed.

"You should try to eat something, Tilly. Don't you go getting sick as well," he said gently as he sat down next to her on the bed and soothingly rubbed her back.

"I can't stay here, Will," she sobbed.

Will nodded, "I know," he said. "I'll look for another room."

"No Will, not just here," she said. "I mean I can't stay in Liverpool, not now. Let's go home to London."

The next afternoon they stood in the rain as they buried their only child. From there they went directly to the station and took the first available train back to London. The journey was made in silence as they grieved for their daughter, and also because they were both worried about what would happen to them next in a city where Will could not find work. The journey was a long one. When they reached Euston, dawn welcomed them. The grief stricken young couple then walked the long miles back to Poplar.

The next day the search for work in London started all over again, but again, none could be found. Word reached him again that there was work to be found in Liverpool, and against Tilly's wishes he made the long walk again. This time, however, work was harder to find. All he was able to find was an odd job here and there. He stayed at the YMCA again. Every letter that he received there from Tilly begged him to return home to London to continue the search for work there. She vowed never to set foot in Liverpool again. At last he agreed, and once again returned to London where the search for work continued. After yet another day of walking the streets he had still found nothing. As he started his journey back home, a cart man drove past going in the direction of Poplar. Will hailed a lift. The cart man stopped. "Where are you going?" he asked.

"Poplar," said Will. "I can't take another step. I've been walking all day looking for work."

"What's your trade?" the cart man asked.

"Cooper," said Will.

"Jump up," the cart man said offering Will his hand to help him up. "You're in luck, my guvnor's looking for a cooper."

"I think I've tried everywhere in Poplar already and nobody is willing to give me work," Will told him. "In fact, I think I've tried pretty much everywhere in London too."

"That's all right, I'll vouch for you," the cart man said. "Anyone that spends his days walking the whole of London looking for work is just fine in my book."

Will sat down next to the cart man and began to laugh heartily. He slapped the cart man on the back and said, "I've spent weeks walking the country looking for a job and now here I am being driven to work triumphantly like the Lord Mayor."

When they arrived at the yard, the cart man told his boss how he had picked Will up walking the streets and looking for work. When Will gave his name, the boss looked a little uneasy, but with the cart man in his corner, Will got the job.

13

At the end of the first week in his new job when Will picked up his wages, he was overjoyed. At last he had a proper job and a regular income again. As he put on his jacket to set off for home, the other workers called to him, "Hey Will, we always go down to the Railway Tavern after work on Saturdays. Come and join us."

"Not me," said Will.

"Why? Won't your missus let you?" they laughed.

"No she won't," Will said seriously. "Besides, I've too often seen the downside of too much alcohol. I've seen people die because of its effects. I've had dead bodies outside my own street door just because some soldiers got drunk and lost control of their senses. Every week I see local men come out of the pubs and stagger home to upset their families. I've lost count of the times that I've seen these drunken men cross paths with other drunken men and end up in fist fights for no reason at all except for the effects of alcohol fueling their aggression. I'm a teetotaler and I intend to stay that way thank you."

One of his new colleagues spoke up, "Don't give people a bad time for going for a drink, Will. A lot of people around here have to live as a whole family in one small room. Is it any wonder that some men need to visit the public house to escape home for a while and drown their sorrows in a pint or two; they have little else in their lives."

Will responded, "Maybe if these men kept their beer money they might be able to afford something better than just one room for their families, or at least put the money to better use, like a new pair of shoes for one of the children, or even better food on the table for the family. It shouldn't just be about what the man wants if there's a whole family that he has to be responsible for." The man just waved off Will's comments and left with the others to go to the pub while Will was met by Tilly, and together they walked home.

The next week at work the men teased Will relentlessly for the fact that he was a teetotaler, but he paid no heed to them and even played along to their playful banter.

"Was that your missus there last week to see you got home without going to the pub first, Will?" one of them joked.

"Yes it was," said Will, "and she'll be there to meet me this week too."

"Oh come on, Will," one of them urged. "Come and have a drink with us after work on Saturday."

Will stuck to his guns and declined their offer again. "I can end the week without a drink thank you very much. I'm not a drinking man and I never will be."
When the next Saturday came around, one of the men discreetly approached him and whispered,
"Hey Will, when you leave today can I walk out with you?"
"Certainly," said Will. "Has your missus been getting at you?"
"Yes," the man said sadly. He looked embarrassed as he added, "The fact is, Will, I stayed drinking down the Railway Tavern last week until I had blown eight shillings. It meant that my two little girls had to go without their new boots that they had been promised."
"All right, Jim, I'll give you a whistle when I'm about to go," said Will. At knocking off time, Will and Jim started walking out together.
"Hey Jim, aren't you coming down the tavern with us?"
"Not tonight lads," Jim said, looking a little guilty as he turned and left with Will.

The following week another of the men, Archie, discreetly approached him. "Hey Will, can I leave with you today?" he asked quietly. "I'm spending far too much money down the Tavern every week, but I usually feel obliged to go when all the other men are going." Will smiled. "I'll give you a whistle when it's time to go," he said. At knocking off time, Will, Jim and now Archie started walking out together.
"Hey Archie, aren't you coming down the tavern with us?"
"Not tonight lads," Archie said as he left with Will and Jim.
At the end of the sixth week not one man from the workshop went to the pub.

One evening after work as he walked out with Jim, his colleague said, "The men have been talking about the high quality of your work, Will."
"Have they now," said Will. "Well Jim, I take enormous pride in anything I create."
"I have a cousin who is a foreman over in Wandsworth. He's looking for a good cooper like you. The money is much better there than what you get here, and he appreciates good quality work too. He keeps asking me to work there, but I've been here too long now and I'm settled in my ways, plus I don't want to trek over to Wandsworth every day. Let me know if you're interested and I'll let him know?"
"I'm very interested, Jim, and I don't mind traveling a long way to work. I'll just wake up earlier in the mornings," Will told him.

Not long afterwards, Will started his new job in Wandsworth. After a few months of working there his new boss approached him. "Why don't you

Where there's a Will, there's a way

move away from Poplar, Will, and take a house nearer to the works?" he asked.

"But suppose you pay me off after the busy period passes," Will said.

"I shan't do that, Will, I like your work too well," his boss said with a smile. "I also know you talk to the men a great deal about the Labour movement and unions too." Will looked surprised. "Oh yes," his boss said knowingly. "I've heard all about your little speeches all right. But I've also never known the rights of the employer observed so honourably. You talk to the men about their rights as workers, but you also talk to them about fairness across the board, and about taking pride in their work. You seem to be able to keep the men more sober and the work up to a higher standard than I have ever seen before. So how about it, Will, why not try to find a house nearer the works. That way I can rest assured that you won't get tired of that long journey from Poplar every day. I don't want you taking a job closer to home."

"I'm quite happy where I live, thank you," was Will's reply.

His boss, however, was right to be concerned, because the chance soon came for Will to take a job closer to home. He was offered a good position in the coopering department of an East London brewery; an offer he couldn't refuse. He was happy to have made the move too. Everything fit into place. He enjoyed the job, respected the company that he worked for, liked the people that he worked with and it was close to home. Now that he felt settled, he began to spend more time studying public affairs and the Labour movement. He was also beginning to be more widely known as a 'Labour agitator'. Just like in his last job, however, he was held in high esteem by the management who valued his good working practices and craftsmanship.

One day while Will was at work, one of his colleagues said, "You know you're getting quite a reputation as a Labour agitator, Will, don't you?"

"Am I?" said Will, sounding unconcerned. His colleague smiled and continued, "I have a few friends over at the docks that would like to hear what you have to say, Will. They say there are others that would be interested in what you have to say too. Would you be interested in talking to them?"

"I would Joe, how about next Sunday?"

"That sounds great, Will. I'll let them know."

"Where shall I go to talk to them?" asked Will.

"Meet us outside the East India dock gates at 10 a.m." said Joe.

14

When Will arrived at the dock gates on Sunday morning, he was quite surprised by the number of people gathered there. Joe was there to meet him and he shook Will's hand. "Thanks for coming, Will," he grinned.

"Not a bad turn out," he added.

"Not a bad turn out at all," said Will, surveying the gathering.

"Here!" said Joe, handing Will a sturdy looking wooden box, "Get up on here."

Will, small and stocky, stepped up onto the box that would make it easier to be seen and cleared his throat. The box was in front of the high brick wall close to the dock gates, so when he stepped onto it he had the wall at his back and his audience in front of him. He spoke loudly and clearly so that everyone could hear him and said, "Well I'm surprised and flattered that so many of you have turned up today. It also pleases me to know that you want to hear about the Labour movement and how by working together we can make a difference to the working man's lot. I'm not just talking about in the workplace either, but in every aspect of our lives. We are the underclass. Why? Because we let ourselves be the underclass, that's why. We chaps are like the old lady's cow that regularly gave a pail of milk, but who then would quite often kick it over. We are creating trade unions and co-operative societies that can be the best working class organisations in the world," he said proudly, "but we have a weakness for kicking the pail over too," he added sadly. "How, you may ask? Well, because we are constantly spoiling our own good work by allowing other classes to do all the governing of this country. It reminds me of a group of boys I saw coming home from a football match once.

'How did you get on?' they were asked by the other lads in the street.

'We won!'

'What was the score?'

'Seven to nil!'

'Have you been playing a blind school?'"

A ripple of laughter went through the audience. He then said seriously, "Well chaps, we workers have been the blind school, and we have been allowing other classes to score goals against us all the time. If we haven't been blind, then we've certainly been blindfolded. It's time to tear that blindfold off I say." His audience applauded politely and when they had finished he carried on. "The Labour movement may be the new force by which God is going to help forward the regeneration of the world. Heaven knows we need a little more earnestness in our national life today, and if the best born cannot give it, then the so called base born may."

More applause.

"We working men are gaining power. Let us see that we also gain knowledge to use that power and not abuse it. Parliament is supposed to protect the weak against the strong. Well it doesn't pan out like that. After all these years of popular education, isn't it about time we taught the dialectical champions in the House of Commons that the people are the creators of Parliament, and that we demand as its creators that Parliament should be at the service of the people, and 'all' of the people, instead of at the service of the powerful and the wealthy."

This brought great applause and people even began cheering and whistling to show their support.

"But don't think that Parliament and municipality can do everything. They are not going to make the world perfect. What they can do and what we should insist on their doing is to make it easier to do right and more difficult to do wrong. They can deal with those 'who turn away the needy from judgment and take away from the poor of my people' as it says in the book of Isaiah, but they cannot make good men and good women. That!" said Will, earnestly, "Must depend upon ourselves."

At the end of his speech, Will received an enthusiastic round of applause and cheers from the men gathered there. Seldom had they heard such words from one of their own. Joe shook his hand vigorously. 'Great speech, Will!" he enthused.

"It did seem to go down well didn't it," agreed Will. "I think I'll come down here again next Sunday too and jump up on my soapbox."

"Well I'll certainly turn out to hear you again," said Joe. "I'll put the word about," he added.

The following Sunday, the audience was even larger; word had obviously spread. Joe was there to meet him again. "A good turn out again, Will," he said smiling. Will also smiled as he nodded agreement.

"They obviously all want to be educated at the Crooks College," said Joe.

"The Crooks College?" asked Will.

"That's what people are calling it," said Joe.

Will chuckled as he gave Joe a friendly pat on the back, "Right then, I suppose I'd better get the College opened." He stepped up onto his box again and addressed his audience. "For those of you good people who were not here last week, just let me tell you what I'm about. I believe in equality and fairness for everyone, regardless of their 'class', but I also believe that the working class needs to help itself and not wait for the so called better classes to treat us as equals. Through Trade Unions and the Labour movement we can make a start, but it also comes down to you people here to take some of that responsibility in making better lives for yourself. Do you see the middle classes and the upper classes down the public houses every weekend drunk out of their skulls? I think not. They have the sense to put their money towards better things in life. For those of you that don't know me, I can tell you that I am a member of the Temperance Society. I do what I can to discourage drinking because I believe it causes far too many problems and hardships in the home and often in the workplace.

Some of you chaps imagine that you can only be men by taking the gargle. If you could see yourselves sometimes after you've been indulging I'm sure you would soon change your opinion. Perhaps you've heard of the drunk who asked for a ticket at the railway station.

'What station?' asked the ticket clerk."

Will acted like a drunk as he said, "'What stations have you got?' the drunk stammered back, clinging to the ledge for support." The crowd laughed.

"But even that chap wasn't as bad as the railway guard who went home drunk and saw the cat lying on the hearthrug. He picked it up, shoved it in the oven, slammed the door, and yelled, 'Take your seats for Nottingham.'"

More laughter as Will imitates the drunken railway guard.

"You all know of the pledge, right?" he asked his audience. "The Temperance movement wants you to stop drinking so we ask that you sign a pledge of total abstinence. Well one day a regular drinker was so drunk that he almost signed himself up for the 'pledge' to stop drinking. He writes his name, puts his hand in his pocket and asks 'How much?'

'Oh there's nothing to pay,' says the young lady from the Temperance Society, smiling.

'What? Nothing to pay?' the drunk repeats in amazement. 'Do I get it for nothing then? Do you mean to say that, I, a working man, am offered something for nothing?'

'Nothing to pay at all,' repeats the young lady happily.

'Well upon my honour, this is the first time that I've ever got anything for nothing. Come and have a drink with me to celebrate.'" Even the drinkers in the crowd laughed.

"Some of you fellows that live on the Isle of Dogs have seen the allotment system started there. I asked one of the publicans of the neighbourhood why he complained about the allotments. 'Why,' he said, 'the men used to come in and have a gargle on Saturday afternoons, but now they go and dig clay.' But ask the men's wives what they say about the allotments and you will hear a different story. The men now have time not only to cultivate their plots, but to look after their families.

How many of our poor women who take to drink can trace their descent to the neglect of the men that married them? It may be hard to be burdened with a drunken wife, but often enough a good deal of the fault is on the side of the husband because of his early neglect. He should have strengthened her. He should have shared her sorrows as well as her joys. We ought not to leave a woman to bear all of her own burdens. Many a young wife breaks down because of early neglect at a time when she ought to be built up, when it would be real manliness on the husband's part to put up with a little trouble for her sake.

Some of you giggle when you see a man carrying a young baby. What is there to giggle at? I carried a baby up the stairs at Shadwell Station the other day, because I saw it was too much for the poor mother struggling alone. 'Here,' I said. 'Hand it over. I'll help.' My wife heard about it before I got home, and she said to those that told her, 'Well if the woman didn't thank him, I shall when he comes home.' Perhaps you think I looked a fool clambering up the stairs with a baby. I didn't think so. I satisfied myself by doing what evidently wanted doing. My good wife and I are lucky to have our own baby daughter, Minnie. Some men think that it's not a man's place to help with the children, but I know different. I know what it feels like to lose a child and I shall do all that I can to help and care for my children, or any others that need caring for, for that matter. I do not see this as making me less of a man; on the contrary, I see this as making me a 'better' man. Don't you see?" he asked his audience imploringly. "To change our lot in life we have to help that change by helping ourselves. That means changing our working class attitudes to become better citizens. Hopefully then, the so called better classes and big companies like the water people will begin to treat us with respect and not take advantage of us.

Here we are again amid another water shortage. So why do we get charged the same when there's no water as we do when there is water? When I got home last night my wife said, 'Will, the water's come on at last, but just look at it, it's not fit to drink'. So I turned on the tap and saw a lot of little things swimming about in the water. The wife was alarmed and asked what we should do. 'My dear,' I replied. 'For goodness sake don't say anything about it to anybody. If this gets to the ears of the water company they might charge us for the fish as well as the water.'"

1878

As Will left the London Hospital one evening late in October after visiting a sick friend, he stepped out onto Whitechapel Road and began the walk back to Poplar. He raised the collar of his coat as a chill wind blew. The smell of smoke filled the air as it drifted down from the chimney pots of the homes that could afford to burn coal. He hadn't gone far when he was startled by two men in uniform as they stepped out of the doorway of a three storied, grey brick building, where lights shone from every floor, lighting up the otherwise dark street outside. The uniforms were not ones that Will recognised. Both men's were different, but they both had the initial 'S' on their high stiff collars. One of the uniforms was a navy blue serge, while the other man wore a scarlet jersey. Both men wore military looking caps, which sported a red band. Although Will did not recognise the uniforms, he did recognise one of the men in them.

"Archie, is that you?" he asked, somewhat puzzled and half expecting the man not to be who he actually thought he was. He was doubly confused because the Archie that he knew was not in the least bit a military type.

"Oh hello, Will!" the man said smiling as he came across to shake Will's hand.

"Have you enlisted?" Will asked, pointing towards the uniform. Archie laughed. "In a manner of speaking I have," he said. "I take it you've heard of William Booth, the preacher?"

"Yes I have," said Will. "He's been creating quite a stir around these parts hasn't he with his sermons for the poor in those large temporary tents that he's been erecting. So you're part of his 'Christian Mission' are you?"

"Actually Will, we've just come from a meeting with him in there," Archie said, indicating the three storied building behind him. "He's decided to change the name from the Christian Mission to the 'Salvation Army'. That's what these new uniforms are all about. He says if we're going to be an army fighting poverty and evil, then we should be dressed like an army. There's only a few of us with uniforms so far, but I'm sure you'll soon see more of them around as the Salvation Army grows in numbers."

Will smiled at this friend. "Well anyone that gives their time trying to help the poor, whether physically or spiritually is a good man by me. I hope your Salvation Army catches on."

Part 2

"The same sun which never set on the Empire, never rose on the dark alleys of East London."

Will Crooks

16

July, 1888

It has been 10 years since Will took the job in the coopering department at the brewery. He's still there happily plying his trade and continues to take great pride in his work. He has also been keeping busy on the home front with the arrival of more children. His daughter, Minnie, now 14, has been joined by his eldest son, Will junior, aged nine; Maggie, aged five; Emily, aged three and one year old, Tilly. The only downside to his home life is the health of his beloved wife, Tilly, who is continually being taken ill.

Will has also continued to develop his interest in the Labour movement and most Sunday mornings he can be found down at the gates of East India Dock in Poplar standing on his wooden podium addressing his loyal audience that has steadily grown over the years. In fact, he has now become quite well known in the area because of his 'College' and his political lectures. Influenced as he was by the speeches of John Bright, Will was also gaining a reputation as a powerful public speaker himself. His own speeches were usually a mix of inspirational evangelistic and comic stories that he often related as personal experiences. On this particular Sunday morning, the sun was already shining brightly overhead. It was shaping up to be a nice, warm July day as Will stepped up onto his podium to get ready to deliver the latest lesson at the Crooks College.

A brief round of applause greeted him and he doffed his hat in response. His black bearded face scanned the crowd of people in front of him. Many of them he knew by name, many just by sight, but all were welcome at the College. When the applause finished and before Will had a chance to utter a word himself, one of the crowd called, "Hey Will! Have you heard that the match girls at Bryant & May over in Bow have gone on strike?"

"Yes I have, Albert," Will told him, "and my thoughts and prayers are with them all. Do any of you men know anybody who works there?" Two men in the crowd raised their hands.

"Just a couple of you I see," said Will. "Well let me tell the rest of you something about what's happened to our neighbours over there in Bow. A good woman by the name of Annie Besant heard a speech at a Fabian Society meeting about the match girls and the conditions those poor women and girls have to work in; such as 14 hour work days, poor pay and excessive fines for the smallest misdemeanor while at work. Did you know that if one of those ladies is just a few minutes late to work in the morning they lose half a day's pay? But the worst of what those poor women have to endure are the severe health problems caused by working with yellow

Where there's a Will, there's a way

phosphorus. Do any of you know of yellow phosphorus?" Just a few of the men raised their hands.

"How about 'phossy jaw' then? Maybe you've heard of that?" Will asked the crowd. This time more men in the crowd nodded and raised their hands that they had.

"For those of you that don't know about phossy jaw, let me tell you all about it. Phossy jaw, gentlemen, is what those poor women and girls over at Bryant & May suffer when exposed to the heated fumes of yellow phosphorus. You know you have phossy jaw when your teeth start to hurt and your gums begin to swell. Your hair then starts to fall out too. Then your jaw bone starts to abscess and becomes extremely painful and then it goes on to disfigure you. The whole side of your face turns green and then black, and if that wasn't bad enough, it would then begin to discharge a foul smelling pus." The men in the crowd looked sickened and a low murmur passed through them as they voiced their disgust. After Will had given them enough time for the horrors of phossy jaw to sink in, he continued.

"And for this, the women and girls at Bryant & May earn just a miserly sum, some of which is regularly lost to the factory's strict fine system. And can you believe that they even have to buy their own tools for cleaning the machinery? When Annie Besant found out about this she wrote an article called 'White slavery in London' for 'The Link' newspaper. The three women that helped Annie with the article have been sacked and this is what has brought about the strike. I fear, however, that without a Union or any proper representation on their behalf, that the employers as usual will get their own way. I ask you all that your thoughts and prayers be with them and their families."

The article in 'The Link' that was written by Annie Besant included the following words: "Born in slums, driven to work while still children, undersized because under-fed, oppressed because helpless, flung aside as soon as worked out, who cares if they die or go on to the streets provided only that Bryant & May shareholders get their 23 percent and Mr. Theodore Bryant can erect statues and buy parks?

Girls are used to carry boxes on their heads until the hair is rubbed off and the young heads are bald at 15 years of age. Country clergymen with shares in Bryant & May's, draw down on your knee your 15 year old daughter; pass your hand tenderly over the silky clustering curls, rejoice in the dainty beauty of the thick, shiny tresses."

When the women and girls (many of them teenagers) started their strike they went to Besant for help. She helped them set up a strike committee and enlisted the support of some newspapers that were sympathetic to their cause, which ran strike funds to support the 1000 or so striking workers. Also under the guidance of Besant, the workers formed a properly constituted trade union and therefore The London Trades Council (a labour organisation that united London's trade unions) got involved on behalf of the match girls. When news spread about the appalling conditions that the women and girls had to work in, they found that public opinion was very much in favour of the workers. It was this overwhelming public support for the match girls that put so much pressure on the directors of Bryant & May.

Two Weeks Into The Strike:

Will lifted his arm and wiped away the sweat on his forehead with the back of his rolled up shirt sleeve. The summer heat made the air inside the yard where he worked hot and uncomfortable. Even with the doors and windows wide open, what little breeze there was did nothing to improve the working conditions. Will picked up a metal band and began to attach it to the bottom of a newly made wooden barrel when he felt a hand on his shoulder. He turned to see one of his colleagues grinning. "Will, have you heard the news?" his colleague asked excitedly. "They won! The match girl's strike is over. The sacked workers have been reinstated and their demands have been met." Will laughed loudly. "Well done ladies!" he then cried.

When the match girls had first walked out, Will had been greatly concerned for them. With no union in place, the only outcome that he could envision back then was that of the defeated women and girls being forced back to work, which in turn would have given Bryant & May even more power to exploit their workers. If Will hadn't had his hands full he would have given his colleague a happy slap on the back for delivering such good news. He felt great joy for the match girls, but also deep within him the flames of another type of joy were beginning to burn. He had spent a good deal of his life preaching the value of Trade Unionism and the rights of the working man; here now was the proof that validated those words. If a group of unskilled workers such as the match girls could form a union and come out on top against a company like Bryant & May, then anybody could do it.

At the next Crooks College, Will, his voice full of passion told his audience, "There's the proof that there's hope for all of us common workers if we just learn to stand together and fight for what's fair and just. All we ask for as employees is a fair wage and fair working conditions in exchange for a fair weeks work. That's not very much to ask for, is it?

Also, I cannot stress enough the importance that public opinion had on the outcome of this particular strike."

When the strike had first begun, few could have imagined a victory for the match girls, but the unlikely success of this group of East End unskilled workers would prove to have far reaching effects; not only in awakening the general public's awareness of the terrible working conditions of some of its fellow citizens at the very heart of the great empire itself, but more importantly it changed the mindset of the working classes themselves and gave them a glimpse of what their power could achieve if they joined together and stood as one.

17

October 4th, 1888

As Will walked towards his home in the early evening after a day at work, he noticed the chill in the air; autumn was here. He saw his children outside playing in the street with their friends. Two of the group of children, a boy and a girl, both in shabby clothing stood facing each other a couple of feet apart clasping each other's hands above their heads making the shape of an arch. The rest of the children stood in a line taking it in turns to walk between the two children making the arch and passing beneath their upturned arms. The two children clasping hands were singing;

> "Oranges and lemons,
> Say the bells of St. Clement's.
>
> You owe me five farthings,
> Say the bells of St. Martin's.
>
> When will you pay me?
> Say the bells of Old Bailey.
>
> When I grow rich,
> Say the bells of Shoreditch.
>
> When will that be?
> Say the bells of Stepney.
>
> I'm sure I don't know,
> Says the great bell of Bow."

Then the children slowed their singing as they sang, "Here comes a candle to light you to bed," and then in a somber tone they sang, "And here comes a chopper to chop off your," and on the last word "head!" the two children forming the arch quickly brought their arms down in a chopping motion to catch the girl currently passing through. The girl screamed in mock horror and the other children screeched with excitement and relief that they were not the one caught.

Will laughed as he watched them all having fun. His eldest daughter, Minnie, who was sitting on the doorstep of their house keeping an eye on

Where there's a Will, there's a way

the younger ones, saw him approaching so she stood up and walked over to meet him. He could see that something was troubling her. "What's wrong?" he asked.

She made sure the other children were out of earshot before saying, "Mother's inside and I think she's upset about something. She was crying earlier."

"Do you have any idea what's wrong?" Will asked, his voice filled with concern.

"No I don't," was her honest reply. "When I asked her if anything was wrong she just said 'no' and then asked me to come out here and keep an eye on the little ones."

"Well you go back to them then and I'll go inside and see what's wrong," he told her.

Inside the house he found Tilly sitting and darning an old worn pair of children's socks. As always now she looked exhausted. "Hello dear," she greeted him. He could see that her eyes were red and that she had been crying. "Is everything all right?" he asked as he removed his coat.

"Oh, I'm just a little shook up," she told him. "Those Whitechapel murders have unnerved me, that's all. I was talking to some of the neighbours earlier and they told me that the police have released a letter that they think is from the murderer and the newspapers published it today. The murderer is calling himself 'Jack the Ripper'. What type of monster is he Will?" she cried as she dabbed at a few more tears that ran down her cheeks. Will went to her and placed a comforting hand on her shoulder and bent to kiss her head. "I saw the letter in the paper myself today," he told her. "You're right to call him a monster," he added.

"Oh Will, it would be bad enough that this sort of thing was happening anywhere, but to think that it's going on here in the East End just makes it seem all the worse. To think that monster might be living amongst us, even here in Poplar has got my nerves all on edge."

"I know," Will said sympathetically. "I've spoken to quite a few people that feel the same way. That letter is only going to increase people's fear around here."

"I just pray the police find the fiend soon before he has a chance to strike again," she said.

"Try not to worry too much about it, Tilly love; I'm sure they'll catch him soon."

18

August 14th, 1889

Will was at work at the brewery when he picked up the wrapped bundle that was his lunch and called across to one of his colleagues. "Hey Fred! I'm just stopping for a bite to eat. I'll be out in the yard if anybody needs me."

"Do you mind if I join you, Will? It looks like a beautiful day out there today."

"Not at all, Fred, come on out."

Fred quickly grabbed his food from his work area and followed Will outside. Once outside they sat on a low brick wall that separated the open yard from the area where the finished barrels were stacked. As Will began to unwrap his food, Fred said, "Hello, who's this?" Will looked up from his food and saw a man in a tatty grey jacket and flat cap walking towards them.

"Will!" called the man. "I've been waiting for you to come outside."

Will realised that he recognised the man as one that he saw regularly down by the docks and who was also a regular at the Crooks College. "Hello John! What are you doing here?" he asked, somewhat puzzled.

"Have you heard the news yet about the Dockers?" John asked. Will had not. "What news is that?" he asked.

"They've gone on strike!"

"What?" cried Will, astonished. "Are you sure?"

"Positive Will. That's where I've just come from. Ben Tillett has led them out."

"Why? What on earth has happened?" asked Will. He was fully aware of the horrendous conditions the Dockers endured, so he realised that something significant must have happened for them to walk out.

"The men were unloading the Lady Armstrong in West India Dock and the company told the men that the plus money was being reduced," John told them.

"What's plus money?" asked Fred as he took a bite of his lunch. John looked at Fred for the first time and said, "Plus money is a bonus that the men get if they unload a ship quickly. Dockers are treated badly enough as it is, but reducing the plus money is the straw that's broken the camel's back." John turned back to Will. "There's a strike committee forming and it's meeting at the Wade Arms in Jeremiah Street. They sent me to ask if you'll attend."

"I certainly will," said Will. "As soon as I leave work I'll go straight there, but it won't be for a few hours yet."

"That's great, Will!" John exclaimed. "I'll tell them that you'll be along later then." He gave a quick nod of his head as a way of goodbye to Fred and left.

When Will arrived at the Wade Arms later that day he was welcomed by Ben Tillett. Tillett had been elected to the post of General Secretary of the Tea Operatives & General Labourers Association two years previously and had even led a previous strike at the Tilbury docks, which had ended in defeat for the dockworkers. He had a handsome, boyish face and his dark hair was swept over in a high wave from left to right.

"Hello Will," he said as he held out his hand and shook Will's in greeting. The two men knew each other already. Tillett had been to more than a few meetings of the Crooks College and he too was a teetotaler and follower of the Temperance Society. Will looked around the table at the other men seated there. He knew most of them, again from the College. He shook hands with Will Thorne from the National Union of Gasworkers & General Labourers; John Burns, a leading socialist and trade unionist and Tom Mann, another leading trade unionist.

"So what on earth happened?" Will asked.

Tillett spoke, "The men approached me yesterday because they were upset about the way their plus money was being paid on the unloading of the Lady Armstrong. The men wanted to strike immediately, but I persuaded them not to and instead contacted the dock authorities about the men's pay and conditions, but when they refused to listen we were then forced to call the strike."

"What are our demands?" asked Will. "Do we have a plan?"

Again it was Tillett that spoke. "Our demands are simple; we want an increase in pay and overtime rates. We're asking for an increase in regular daytime pay from fivepence per hour, to sixpence per hour, and an increase in overtime pay from sevenpence per hour to eightpence per hour."

"Do we know what the mood of the dock owners is now that the men have gone on strike? Do you think they'll budge?" Will asked. Tom Mann spoke up. "Once they get over the shock that the men have actually walked out, I'm guessing they are going to be pretty stubborn and not give an inch. It's the way they usually operate after all."

"I can vouch for that," said Tillett.

"Will," said Thorne. "We've all heard you speak down by the dock gates; you have a way of moving people with your words. People listen to you and you get your message across. This is a momentous day, no doubt about that, but we have no money. If the dock owners don't give in to our demands immediately, which I think we all know won't happen, then we need to raise money, and fast, to help feed the striking dock workers and their families." Will nodded. "I follow you," he said. "I'll start straight away. I'll also return here again tomorrow after work to check in for updates."

As Will left he called over one of the striking Dockers from the crowd that was outside the Wade Arms. "Do me a favour will you?" Will asked. "I'm about to go out to try and raise some money for you men, but I haven't been home from my own work yet. Could you pay a visit on my wife and let her know what's happening and that I won't be home till late tonight."

"Sure, I'll do that for you." the man replied, so Will gave the man his address. When the messenger had left, Will looked around at the faces of the striking Dockers gathered there and noticed John, the man who had brought him the news earlier in the day." Hello again John," said Will. "I'm about to go out to try to raise some money for the strikers and their families. Do you fancy joining me?"

"I'd love to, Will," John replied.

"Great! Do you know anyone else that will join us? As I'm representing the Dockers it makes sense to have a few with me. That way people will see the human aspect of the strike too."

"I know quite a few good men that will come along," said John. "Just give me a few minutes to speak to them."

Will and his band of striking Dockers walked around the corner onto East India Dock Road and then headed for Commercial Road. At that time of the day the pavements were busy with workers on foot returning home for the evening, and horse drawn omnibuses and carriages filled the streets.

On both sides of the street stood a mish-mash of connecting three and four storied buildings, which were a mixture of shops and homes; the shops with their awnings pulled down to protect their goods and their customers from the late summer sun. The side of the street that Will headed for was the busier side due to the fact that it now sat in shade. The smell of horses and their droppings filled the warm summer air.

At every major road junction, or where any people were gathered, Will stood on the wooden beer crate that he had borrowed from the Wade Arms and called on passers-by to stop and listen to what he had to say. When Will started his address, shopkeepers and residents also came out to see what the commotion was all about from this short black bearded man with the bellowing voice.

"Ladies and Gentlemen!" he began. "You may have already heard the momentous news that the dock workers have gone on strike. You may have even thought that the news was just a false rumour. Well my friends here with me, all of them dock workers are here to tell you that those rumours are true. These fine, honest and hardworking men, for so long down trodden by the dock owners, and also for the most part treated as nothing more than animals have at last said 'No More!'

I myself am not a dock worker, but years ago when I was desperate for work I found myself down at the dock gates in the hope of finding work, but what I found there turned my stomach ladies and gentlemen. I have never seen men so desperate to work, yet treated so badly. I was sickened by the plight of these poor wretched fellows; so sickened in fact that I fled that place in a daze.

Let me tell you about the call-on as I have experienced it. When I arrived at the dock gates I was at once shocked by the amount of men gathered there waiting for the foreman to call on the lucky ones that he favoured for a few hours work that day. When the foreman appeared, the gathered men lunged forward pushing others out of their way as they scrambled to get to the front. I saw men fall and then get trampled as the crowd relentlessly pushed forward. I also stood and watched in horror as these desperate men came to blows as they fought to get into view of the foreman. Believe me when I say I felt sick to my stomach witnessing the crowd's desperation. The sight was enough for me to see only once in my lifetime for the events to stay etched in my memory, but these poor people have to endure the call-on, two or three times each day.

The dock owners have treated these men with contempt and caused them and their families to live in abject poverty. It's a disgrace that we are living in the Capital city of our great empire, yet we make our own decent men and their families live and work in such conditions. It is shameful I tell you.

Now to their demands; all they are asking for is sixpence per hour during their regular daytime shift, which is just one penny more than what they receive now, and also one penny more on their overtime rates, which would increase their overtime rate to eightpence per hour. Bear in mind, however, that because of the call-on, they may actually only get three hours of work that day, as there is no guarantee that the men will get work at the second call-on just because they had already worked that day. I'm here this evening to bring your awareness to these issues and ask that you support these poor fellows as best you can. Striking means no money at all for any of the striking men. If you support them in what they are doing, please give anything you can to help them through this most difficult of times. My friends here will pass among you good people, please give what you can."

The striking men moved through the small crowd and held out their flat caps and people that could afford to, placed money in them. When the crowd dispersed, Will picked up the crate and they set off down the road until they came to the next major junction and repeated the process. They were raising money, but Will knew that they would need a lot more than this. When he returned home that night it was almost midnight. He quickly ate and went to bed. Tilly lay in bed asleep. She looked very pale and drawn. She was carrying her seventh child (including daughter Matilda that had died as a baby in Liverpool) and was currently eight and a half months pregnant. Will quietly climbed into bed beside her, snuggled up and fell soundly asleep.

The next morning he was up bright and early and off to work. After his day of work was over he headed straight to the Wade Arms and met with Ben Tillett and the other men leading the strike.

"Great work last night, Will," they said. "You brought in a nice amount." Will, however, did not look happy and said seriously, "I'm afraid we're going to need a lot more than that. I'll be off again soon to see what we can raise tonight." He then changed the subject, "So what news of the strike?" Tom Mann answered, his top lip almost hidden beneath a large thick moustache with pointed waxed ends. Mann was 33 years old and when he spoke, his accent reflected his midlands origins, "Good news and bad, Will. The good news is that the Stevedores have gone on strike in sympathy." He gestured along the table. "This is Tom McCarthy, head of the Stevedores union; he led them out." Will could hardly believe what he was hearing. The Stevedores coming out in support was incredible news.

The docks had their own type of class system between the different groups of workers there with the Stevedores sitting comfortably at the top. Their work was essential for the docks to function. They already had a very strong union and received good rates of pay. For them to be making a stand in support of the unskilled workers at the very bottom of the dock's class system was a major coup for the strike organisers. Will leant across the table and shook Tom's hand. Tom was another that he knew from the Crooks College.

"As you know," Mann continued, "The Stevedores carry high status in the port and their work is essential to the running of the docks. We're also trying to get support from other workers in and around the docks like the Lightermen and Watermen."

"It's great to have you with us, Tom." Will said, beaming.
John Burns pushed a sheet of paper across the table to Will. "Here's a statement just released by Tom on behalf of the Stevedores union to the press; it's good. Will picked up the sheet of paper and read;

Where there's a Will, there's a way

"To the Trade Unionists and People of London.

Friends and fellow Workmen. The dock labourers are on strike and asking for an advance in wages ... sixpence per hour daytime and eightpence per hour overtime. The work is of the most precarious nature, three hours being the average amount per day obtained by the docker. We, the Union of the Stevedores of London, knowing the conditions of the dock labourers, have determined to support their movement by every lawful means in our power... We now appeal to members of all trade unions for joint action with us, and especially those whose work is in connection with shipping - engineers and fitters, boiler makers, ships' carpenters, etc. and also the coal heavers, ballast men and Lightermen. We also appeal to the public at large for contributions and support on behalf of the dock labourers."

Will nodded in appreciation and congratulated Tom McCarthy on the document and then turned back to Tom Mann and asked, "So what's the bad news?"

"Charles Norword is acting as the spokesperson for the dock companies and it appears that he has no intention of giving an inch." Will sighed. "We have to get the public on our side like the match girls did to put added pressure on the dock companies," he said. "If we let the nation see just how badly these men are treated, I'm sure we'll also be able to raise enough money to see us through too."

"I've been thinking the same thing!" said Tillett. "I propose we organise some marches from the East End down to Tower Hill and even into the City itself; well organised though and peaceful. When Londoners see that these are just normal men trying to earn a fair wage to support their families we'll hopefully win over that public support." The other strike leaders agreed that this was a good idea. Tom Mann said, "Let's make a real procession out of it if we can. Let's try to get families involved too, with carriages for the young ones and wives walking alongside their husbands so that people can see the human aspect of the strike."

"Great idea!" said Burns. "We can get them to carry hats, buckets, bags or anything else that can hold money and hopefully collect donations along the way. This could be a great opportunity to not only win public support, but raise some much needed relief money."

"Hear! Hear!" was the chorus of approval around the room. Will then changed the subject and asked, "Have we released our own statement of our demands yet?"

"Yes!" replied Tillett. "It appeared in most of today's newspapers. We've told them that we want a wage of sixpence per hour and a raise in the overtime rates. We also want the Contract and Plus systems abolished and call-ons to be reduced to two a day. We're also demanding that the men be taken on for a minimum of four hours at a time."

"Good stuff," said Will. "Well then gentlemen, I'm off again with some of the men to try and raise more money. I'll see you again tomorrow."

The next day 20,000 men, including the seamen, the firemen, the lightermen and watermen joined the dockers on strike and the entire dock was now out. Will's day was a repeat of his previous two; awake early for work at the brewery, then off to check in with the other leaders at the Wade Arms and then off to raise more money for the strikers and then finally getting home again after midnight.

Just before midday on August 21st, a large seething mass of people that included the striking dock workers, their wives, their children and supporters crammed into the streets surrounding West India Docks. Many stared around in amazement at the sheer number of people gathered there, while mothers tried to keep their children in check and others put finishing touches to the horse drawn floats, which hung banners declaring the professions that the individual floats represented.

As the marchers set off, led as they were by a Brass Band, they made their way through the East End to Tower Hill. The 20,000 or so people that made up the procession chanted as they walked, "A fair wage for fair work!" and "Support the Dockers!" Many waved colourful flags, while others carried homemade effigies of the dock owners. Behind the band walked a docker holding aloft a long wooden pole. At its tip a children's doll dressed in dirty rags had been attached. Beneath the doll hung a sign, which read, 'A dockers child'. The thousands of marchers that were waiting patiently in the side streets then slowly began to filter through into the main body of the procession, like many small veins feeding the main artery. As they marched they sang the following; a popular nursery rhyme that was altered especially to be sang on the march:

"Sing a song of sixpence,
dockers on the strike.
Guinea pigs as hungry,
as the greedy Pike.
Till the docks are opened,
Burns for you will speak.
Courage lads, and you'll win,
well within the week."

Anything the marchers could carry that would hold donations they held out for the people lining the streets to throw money into. The procession was quite a spectacle and the Londoners that stood and watched applauded and cheered as it passed. When they reached Tower Hill, Tillett, Will, and the charismatic 'man in the straw hat' as he was known, John Burns, were among those that gave rousing speeches. The march was a great success. Not only did it raise a great deal of money for the strikers and win over a lot of public support, but it also went a long way towards galvanizing the strikers themselves.

When Will next met with the rest of the strike committee, they delivered some bad news. Tom Mann's fears that Norwood and the rest of the dock employers were not going to give in easily to the dock worker's demands were realised. It was obvious they planned to starve the dockers into submission.

"They're bringing in Blacklegs," Will was told.

"We need to organise pickets then," Will replied.

Tillett agreed. "We were just discussing how to go about that," he said.

"Well we have an army of men at our disposal," said Will.

"Then we should organise them like an army," said Burns. "We need to be well disciplined and well behaved so that we can keep public favour, but we need the pickets to be out in large enough numbers to deter the Blacklegs. They'll be more intimidated by a large crowd and more likely to heed our message of not crossing the picket line then." The committee then decided on a system just like the army hierarchy of Generals, Captains and Sergeants that would organise and mobilise the men as their own army of picketing foot soldiers.

After he left the meeting, Will went off again with some of the striking dockers to try to raise more money. Once again it was some time after midnight before he returned home to his bed, and then again the next morning he was up and off to work as usual at the brewery. At the end of his shift, Will again headed for the Wade Arms and discussed the latest developments regarding the strike.

The committee decided that the best way to distribute the funds that were collected was to create a voucher system. The vouchers were to be given to the striking families where local shopkeepers would then exchange them for food. It was a good thing too as the morning papers carried the news that the dock employers showed no sign of weakening their stance. Mr. Holland, Chairman of the Dock Directors was quoted as saying, "We cannot afford an advance in wages, for it would either destroy any possibility of dividend to the shareholders of the joint companies or tend to drive shipping from the port. When the pinch comes, as come it must, the hopes of the strikers will receive a severe shock and I shall be surprised if there is any backbone left."

10 days into the strike and the marches continued; donations poured in and when Will wasn't at his own work or at the Wade Arms he was out trying to raise further funds with his fund raising rallies. He was tired and drained of energy, but he still carried on with his grueling schedule, uncomplaining. When he arrived at the Wade Arms one evening after going there straight from work again he almost fell into his chair. He put his elbows on the table in front of him and rubbed at his sore, tired eyes. John Burns passed a newspaper over to him; it was the East London Advertiser. "There's a good piece in here today about the latest march, Will," he said. Will picked up the newspaper and read:

"It was impossible not to admire the self-control of those who could in ten minutes have sacked every shop within a mile and satisfied the craving of nature. Contrast this crowd with the French mob which cried hoarse with passion "Give us bread!" Not so the English docker, independent still in his direst straits. "Give me work!" he says and in this case a rider is added and "Pay me fairly!" That is the grit of the whole matter, a fair wage."

After he finished reading he had to rub his eyes again, already red with tiredness.

"Will, are you getting enough rest?" asked Burns.

"I'm fine," said Will, shrugging off the question.

"Well you don't look fine," said Burns, sounding concerned. "Why don't you take a night off and get some rest. You're working your regular day job, and then coming here to help with the organising and administrative work. I know you've been here some mornings too before you even go to your own job, and I hear you're out past midnight every night trying to raise funds. We're all committed to the cause, Will, but you're doing too much. Don't make yourself ill." Will looked slightly affronted by this suggestion. "Not while those poor men and their families are out there close to starving. I'll raise every penny I can for them until I drop. Besides, I hear you've been at it all day and night too, so you're a fine one to talk."

"Yes, but I don't have a pregnant wife at home," Burns said.

"And nearly due," added Will. "But she backs me in this, John. She knows what's at stake."

August 26th, 1889. Evening News & Post

"Dockmen, lightermen, bargemen, cement workers, carmen, ironworkers and even factory girls are coming out. If it goes on a few days longer, all London will be on holiday. The great machine by which five millions of people are fed and clothed will come to a dead stop, and what is to be the end of it all? The proverbial small spark has kindled a great fire which threatens to envelop the whole metropolis."

Where there's a Will, there's a way

The marchers set off on another procession, this time from Poplar to Temple Bar in the City of London. Once again the colourful procession with its marchers and floats lit up the streets; its tens of thousands of marchers singing as they walked, accompanied by many marching bands. As usual thousands of people lined the streets cheering them on. When they reached Aldgate, the boundary that marked the divide between the East End and the City, the leading marchers were met by a line of policemen blocking the road. The marches had all been peaceful and the police up until now had kept their distance. In England, open-air meetings and processions were not illegal, and there was no law to stop people collecting money in the streets, so as no laws had been broken, the police kept their distance while keeping a close eye on proceedings to make sure order was kept, which of course it was. As the procession came to a halt, news spread through it that the police were blocking the route and silence befell the marchers.

"Is there a reason why we can't pass?" asked one of the leading marchers. "Our marches are always peaceful."

A burly looking red haired policeman stepped forward, his face covered in a fiery red beard "It's my duty to inform you that unreasonable noise such as the playing of loud music and loud singing within the City boundaries is against the law. The law is there to protect the inhabitants of the City."

"Can I whistle then?" asked another one of the marchers as he stepped forward.

"Well I don't know of a law that prohibits whistling," replied the police officer.

"So I can whistle too then?" asked another of the marchers.

"Well I don't see why not," the officer replied.

When the marchers promised that the band would not play within the City boundaries and that the marchers themselves would not sing, the line of policemen moved aside and the marchers were allowed to set off again. The two men at the front of the procession then began to whistle as they walked and were quickly joined by others. The whistling then spread out like ripples throughout the length of the procession. Soon the whole procession was whistling 'The Marseilles' as they marched through the old city streets. The bystanders that witnessed the event could not help but be moved by the sound of more than 20,000 people whistling as one as they marched.

August 27th, 1889

130,000 workers were now estimated to be on strike, with new strikes breaking out daily throughout the Capital. One of the most common banners on the marches read, 'Out of principle'. It appeared that most of London was now adopting that point of view. If it wasn't there already, then London was heading for a full-on general strike. The Capital city was shutting down.

19

The striking workers and their families continued the marches, but on almost empty stomachs this was becoming harder each time. The marches now did little to lift morale. The donations coming in were just not meeting the needs of the striking families. Most had already sold or pawned what little they owned to buy food. Organisations such as the Salvation Army and church missions had opened soup kitchens to supply free meals to the hungry, but the fact was that by the end of August, many Dockers and their families were starving. If the strike continued for much longer, the dock owners would get their way and will have starved the men into submission.

After work, Will quickly popped in to the Wade Arms for an update. "I hear you're actually taking the evening off," said Tom Mann who was busy making relief plans with John Burns' wife, Charlotte, along with Eleanor Marx, (the daughter of Karl Marx) who was a friend of Ben Tillett (Eleanor had also helped Annie Besant during the Match Girls strike).

"Yes," said Will. "The wife is about to give birth to our 6th child anytime now so I need to be there."

After a quick update from the other strike leaders, Will dashed home. When he arrived home and opened his street door he heard the sound of a baby crying. His mother came out of the bedroom smiling happily as Will approached. "Congratulations!" she said hugging him tightly. "You have another son!"

Will went into the bedroom to see Tilly and his new son. His other children were already there too. The youngest ones couldn't wait to tell him that mother had had a baby. Will feigned surprise at the news. "Well let me take a look then," he said excitedly. He smiled at Tilly. She looked dreadfully weak. She had been ill during most of the pregnancy, but she was smiling happily now.

"Our little dock strike baby," she said as she pulled down the shawl a little so that Will could see his new son's face.

"Well hello, George," he said as he bent over and took his new son from his wife's arms. He sat down on the bed next to Tilly and was joined by some of the children. Will filled them all in on the latest from the strike. It felt good to be able to spend some valuable time with his wife and children again.

He had been home for a couple of hours when there was an urgent sounding knocking at the street door. Both Will and Tilly heard Will's mother go to the door. "We need Will Crooks," a man's voice cried excitedly. Will looked at Tilly.

"Go Will," she said. "Never let it be said your wife kept you from helping those in need."

"I'll just see what the commotion is and then I'll be back," he told her.

When Will approached the street door, he saw two men standing on his doorstep. When they saw him approach one of them said excitedly, "We're sorry to interrupt you, Will, but the strike committee sent us. The Australians are sending us money. Their workers have raised £30,000 for us."

"£30,000!" Will exclaimed, rubbing his black beard thoughtfully. He then laughed heartily. "This is turning out to be a good night."

"We won't starve now, Will," said the other man at the door.

"No you won't!" agreed Will.

The promised money soon began to pour in from Australia. It now seemed unlikely that the striking men would be starved into submission anytime soon and the advantage was put back into the hands of the strikers. The scent of victory was now in the air. However, even with this news the dock companies remained stubborn, much to the annoyance of the ship-owners and wharfingers who wanted action taken immediately to end the strike. The ship-owners were now even talking openly about unloading the ships themselves.

On a train traveling from Charing Cross to New Cross, Jim Connell, originally from Kilskyre in County Meath, Ireland, but who had lived in London since 1875, had just attended a lecture on socialism at a meeting of the Social Democratic Federation. He was so inspired by the lecture and by the sacrifices of the dock workers in their stand against the dock owners, as well as activities at home of the Irish Land League, that he wrote a song that would quickly become the anthem of the international Labour movement. "The people's flag is deepest red," it began. Even today that red flag is still flying as the official anthem of the British Labour Party.

September 5th, 1889

With no end to the strike in sight and the prospect of all of London coming to a standstill, the Lord Mayor of London, James Whitehead, took action and invited both sides of the dispute to the Mansion House to try to resolve the issue.

Back at the Wade Arms, the strike committee met to weigh up the offer from the Lord Mayor. They decided unanimously to send Ben Tillett and John Burns to represent the dock workers. The good news was that the Roman Catholic Archbishop of Westminster, Cardinal Manning, was to be a mediator at the Mansion House meeting too. Although the Cardinal had family connections to the shipping industry, he had already shown that his sympathies were with the dock workers and their families, many of whom were Catholics. Although his sympathies were with the dock workers, as Roman Catholic Archbishop of Westminster, he was respected by both sides. At the end of the Wade Arms committee meeting, Tillett assured everyone gathered there "That there was no margin for concession. We have made no extravagant demands." As one, the strike committee stood and applauded.

The Cardinal was a tall man and he stood out from the rest of the committee in his red cassock and zucchetta. He was also a blessing for the dock workers. He endorsed their demands with a suggestion of authority, but when it was needed, he used remarkable diplomacy. He was also subtle when subtlety was called for, and was ever courteous to all parties concerned.

On September 7th, the breakthrough finally came and the dock companies reluctantly agreed to the increase in wages and met the main demands of the workers:

* No man to be taken on for less than four hours ensuring a minimum wage of two shillings.
* The abolition of sub-contracting in favour of piecework with the minimum wage of sixpence an hour, or eightpence for overtime; overtime being from 6 p.m. to 6 a.m.

The only item now to decide on was when the new regulations were to come into force.
The dock companies suggested January 1st.
The dock workers rejected that date and suggested October 1st.
The dock companies rejected that date and then suggested December 1st.
The dock workers then rejected that date and in turn suggested November 4th, the first Monday of the month. Both sides finally agreed. The dock workers then agreed to return to work on September 16th.

On September 15th, one last great celebratory procession took place. The victorious dock workers marched to Hyde Park, where a huge victory celebration took place. It was no surprise that the flag of the Australian colonies took pride of place.

20

As the news sank in that the strike was finally over and that the dock workers had won their historic battle, Will's body finally rebelled against the strain that it had been put under during the weeks of the strike. When he collapsed and was rushed to the London Hospital on Whitechapel Road, his friends and family feared the worst. He was completely exhausted and lay close to death. Only after a struggle of 13 weeks was he pronounced out of danger.

One day as he lay in his hospital bed recovering; feeling happy that he was now regaining some of his strength and would soon be able to go home again, he noticed a man of the cloth going from bed to bed within the ward. When he reached Will's bed he asked quite bluntly, "Are you a miserable sinner?"

"No," said Will. "I may be a sinner, but I am not a miserable one right now."

The clergyman scoffed and stormed off in disgust, although a short time later when he had calmed down he approached Will again and asked, "Would you allow me to send you a testament?"

"Certainly," agreed Will. "You are more than welcome to do that."

A few days later, Will received the testament. He opened it and noticed that in several places underlined in red ink, it showed places that were obviously highlighted to show what a depraved and miserable creature he was. The next day the clergyman visited the ward again and came over to Will.

"Hello," he said gravely. "Did you receive the testament?"

"I did, thank you," Will acknowledged.

"And did you notice the marked passages?"

"I did, thank you," repeated Will.

"And what did you think of them may I ask?" the clergyman asked. Will was honest and said, "As applied to me, they are not true."

"What?" exclaimed the clergyman, obviously not amused. He gave Will a withering look, then turned and again stormed off in disgust. A few minutes later after the clergyman had left, another one of the patients on the ward came over to Will. "I say, Will," the man said laughing, "That's the way to get rid of them." Will couldn't help but laugh himself. "How did you get rid of him?" he asked the man.

"He just asked me if I was a miserable sinner, so I said 'yes I am' and he said 'Thank god for that!' and left."

A few days later, Will awoke in his hospital bed after a short nap to find some of the patients and a nurse peering out of one of the large windows.

"What's going on out there?" he asked.

"There's a couple of fancy carriages out there and some even fancier looking toffs," said one of the patients. The nurse gasped, "Upon my soul! I've never seen such a beautiful dress. Just look at how beautiful the woman is wearing it too. I bet she's a Lady or a Duchess or something just as glamorous."

"I expect they're here to see me," joked Will.

"Not bloody likely mate," said one of the patients that had part of his head bandaged. "They're here to see 'him' aren't they?"

The others fell silent.

"Him?" asked Will.

The nurse said, "He means our special guest."

Will still looked puzzled.

The man with the bandaged head then said, "You know, that Elephant Man person from the freak shows that they have living here."

"Really Mr. Smith," the nurse scolded. "He has a name you know, bless his poor soul; it's John Merrick."

21

When Will had fully recovered and was back on his feet, the full force of the dock workers victory and its implications began to hit home. He was sure it was the beginning of a new era in labour relations and the rights of the working man. He desperately wanted to be involved in pushing for change and the advancement of socialism. The Fabian society; a British intellectual socialist movement whose purpose was to advance the principles of socialism was just what Will was looking for, so he decided to join them.

The Fabian society had been founded in London in 1884. It was in fact an offshoot of a group called the Fellowship of the New Life. The Fellowship wanted to transform society by setting an example of clean simplified living for others to follow. They favoured gradual change in society rather than revolutionary change. However, some members also desired to be more politically involved in society's transformation, hence the creation of a separate group, the Fabian society. The writer, George Bernard Shaw was already a Fabian, as was Annie Besant (from the Match Girls strike) and J Ramsay MacDonald (who would go on to become the UK's first ever Labour Prime Minister).

The Fabian society usually held its meetings every two weeks and Will was a regular attendee. At these meetings and lectures, papers on social subjects were read and discussed, along with proposed political and social reforms. At the core of the Fabian society were Sidney and Beatrice Webb. Together they wrote numerous studies of industrial Britain, including alternative co-operative economics that applied to ownership of capital as well as land. British suffragette leader, Emmeline Pankhurst would also join the Fabian society shortly after Will.

1891

It was early afternoon on a warm summer's day, but Tilly lay in bed resting. Will brought in a small damp towel and placed it carefully on her forehead.

"Thanks Will," she said quietly as she forced a smile. She had still not recovered from her previous illness and of the worry of Will being in the hospital for so long after the dock strike. Having six children to cope with too robbed her of any remaining energy.

"Here, I've brought you some tea too," Will said. "Would you like me to pour you some?" he asked.

"Oh yes please, Will," she said gratefully.

He helped her sit up and placed her pillow behind her back for support. She held the towel to her forehead with one hand while she took the cup of tea from Will in the other. Just as she took the cup there was a loud knock on the street door. Satisfied that Tilly was comfortable, Will left her side to go and see who it was. When he opened the door, two men stood on the doorstep and introduced themselves as members of the Poplar Labour League.

"We have a proposal for you that we hope you'll be interested in," one of the men said.

"Well come on in then," said Will. "I've just made a pot of tea if you'd like some."

"That would be nice, thank you," they replied as Will showed them into the sitting room. The men sat down and as Will poured them tea, he asked, "So what is this proposal gentlemen?"

"Look Will," said one of the men. "With your work at your College at the dock gates, along with the role you played in the dock strike, the Poplar Labour League believe you can be a lot more useful in public life than at a workman's bench. We want you to run for a seat on the London County Council."

After the 1886 General Election, the Conservative Government made plans to reform local government. The 1888 Local Government Act created 66 county councils. Councilors were to be elected by household suffrage and serve as councilors for three years. The London County Council (LCC) came into being in 1889. The LCC was the first metropolitan wide form of general local government. These councils became responsible for the management of roads, bridges, drains and general county business. As a result of this legislation, London became a separate county with its own form of government.

The man talking added, "If you agree, then we'd want you to give up your job at the brewery so that you would be able to represent us full time. In return we'd pay you a sum that is equal to your present salary."

"Gentlemen, I'm honoured that you place that much faith in me," Will said humbly.

"So you'll do it?" the men asked.

Will paced back and forth as he considered the offer. At last he stopped and said, "All right, if you wish it, but as soon as you tire of me, no grumbling behind my back. Come forward and say so plainly and I'll go back to the workbench at once." The two men were elated. "Thank you, Will!" they exclaimed as they shook his hand. "Plans are already in place for the creation of the 'Will Crooks Wages Fund'. As soon as you give up the workbench we'll start paying you from the fund."

1892

In the chilly months leading up to the London County Council election that was being held in early March, Will was busy campaigning for a place on the council. From home to home and workplace to workplace he took his campaign message. At trade union meetings, church meetings and street meetings he spoke of his plans for Poplar and London as a whole.

At the Crooks College on a cold and overcast Sunday morning, Will stood on his podium with the collar of his coat upturned and spoke to the large crowd that was gathered there. Part of his speech that day included his election pitch: "People of Poplar, I ask for your vote to help put me on the London County Council. As a workman I should seek especially to represent the interests of the working classes who form three-fourths of the ratepayers of Poplar, while giving every attention to the general work of the London County Council and to the general interests of Poplar.

I am heartily in favour in what is known as the London programme – of home rule for London, as enjoyed by other municipalities; of the relief of the present ratepayers by taxing the owner as well as the occupier; and of the equalisation of rates throughout London for the relief of the poorer districts.

I am in favour of municipal ownership or control of water, tramways, markets, docks, lighting, parks, and the police and I would support all measures which would help to raise the standard of life for the poor, especially in the way of better housing and a strict enforcement of the Public Health Acts."

In March, 1892, Will was elected to the LCC with a large majority. Also returned for the second time was his dock strike companion John Burns who had first been elected to the LCC in the same year as the dock strike. There were enough working men returned to the LCC that the LCC Labour Party was formed and it was agreed that Burns would be its leader. On April 26th, 1892, Will, Burns and the other small band of Labour councilors met at the offices of the Dockers Union on Mile End Road and laid out their radical new policy. In the small, dingy room, these pioneers of Labour put fourth their plans, which included creating a LCC works department.

At the top of the elliptical spiral staircase of the council building at Spring Gardens stood the main floor which housed the horseshoe-shaped council chamber where members were currently debating the finer points of the introduction of the new works department. The Labour members want to introduce a fair wages clause to protect the workers that are being hired directly by the new department. The debate has now been running for most of the day and many council members are ready to vote and accept the policy as it stands, which is without a fair wages clause, but this is most unsatisfactory for the Labour bench.

"No! no! no!" cried Burns as he thumped his fist down on the heavy wooden table in front of him in frustration. "The Labour members of this council simply cannot accept things as they are. We feel that the policy the chamber is about to adopt falls far short of protecting the workers employed by the LCC."

From the other side of the room a Moderate member responded, "Mr. Burns, the way the policy is laid out now is the most reasonable version that the council can accept and now I call for that policy to be voted upon and accepted."

"Just one moment please," pleaded Will as he hastily started scribbling on a sheet of paper laid out before him. When he had finished writing, he passed the paper to Burns to read. As soon as Burns had finished reading it, he stood up, and as the leader of the Labour bench said, "Gentlemen, I move that we add this amendment to the policy. This is our new fair wages clause." He then read the following to the room:

"That all contractors be compelled to sign a declaration that they pay the trade union rate of wages and observe the hours of labour and conditions recognised by the London Trade Unions, and that the hours of labour be inserted in and form part of the contract by way of schedule, and that penalties be enforced for any breach of agreement."

The chairman, Lord Rosebery, addressed Burns, "Could you please pass that around the chamber so that we can all take a few minutes to read and absorb it."

"Certainly," agreed Burns, smiling broadly. As the piece of paper was passed around the chamber he turned to Will and whispered, "Now that was a happy inspiration."

When the other council members had passed around the clause the objections soon began. A leading moderate member took the floor and exasperated said, "But to enforce Trade Union wages would be to fly in the face of political economy."

Will stood and responded passionately, "Political economy, sir, unfortunately never took humanity into account, but unless humanity is considered there can be no justice to the worker. No contractor has ever been ruined by paying Trade Union rates of wages. The best wages has always meant the best workmen. So in the name of humanity and Christianity I appeal to the council to adopt Trade Union wages."

As Will sat back down, Lord Rosebery, the chairman spoke, "It's getting late gentlemen. I'm going to adjourn the meeting. Hopefully we'll make some progress on this tomorrow." However, the debate went on for week after week with no signs of a resolution in sight. Finally Lord Rosebery advised the council that he was going to call a special meeting to decide the issue once and for all.

On the day of the special meeting, Will received a request from Lord Rosebery to join him in his office 30 minutes before the meeting began to discuss the clause that was causing so much trouble. As Will entered the office, two of the moderate members of the council that were opposed to the fair wages clause stopped to comment as they saw Will enter. As one of them patted the other on the back in congratulatory style, he said, "Don't worry old chap, his Lordship will soon put the upstart in his place."

"Yes indeed," said the other, smiling. "I'm sure he will."

Inside his office, Lord Rosebery welcomed Will. "Please sit down," he said pointing to a chair on the other side of his neatly arranged desk. Will thanked him and sat down. He looked across at his lordship's clean shaven and soft featured face. He was still only in his mid-forties, but the eyes that looked back across the desk at Will were bright and brimming with intelligence and confidence. Will, not one to be intimidated, held his gaze and patiently waited for his lordship to speak. He could not know it then, but in less than two years the man sitting across from him would be leading the country as Prime Minister. However, in spite of the confidence in Lord Rosebery's eyes, Will noticed that he shifted just a little uneasily in his chair before saying, "Look here, Crooks, we need to get this matter sorted

Where there's a Will, there's a way

out as it's taking up far too much of the council's time. Now how about you withdraw your claim for Trade Union wages......"

When the special meeting began, the two moderate members that had witnessed Will's summoning were busy congratulating themselves and spreading the news to the others on their side of the debate when Lord Rosebery called the meeting to order. "Right then gentlemen, we are here today as you know with the aim of resolving this one stumbling block; the fair wages clause. I would like to suggest that we accept the clause and ask for your backing in this."

The two moderate members that were just celebrating audibly gasped. "Really Mr. Chairman?" asked one of them, clearly confused. "Are we to believe that you now favour this clause?"

"Yes sir, I do," his lordship replied. "I've discussed it in detail with Mr. Crooks and he delivers a very strong case and I now believe that this clause should be included."

Sir Thomas Farrer then stood and said, "Well then Mr. Chairman, if this clause is to be included I would like to suggest that we change the wording from 'London' to 'In the place or places where the contract is executed'."

"That seems like a good amendment, Sir Thomas," Lord Rosebery said. "I have an amendment of my own too, one that will remove any difficulty for the council deciding wages in unforeseen cases. My amendment is that 'Rates of pay are to be not less, nor the hours of labour more than those recognised by associations of employers and trade unions and in practice obtained'. Please get that added and get the full version circulating in the chamber so that we can review what we have and take a vote." When the vote was taken, the Bill, which now had the chairman's backing was passed. It was to be Will's first of many successes at the LCC.

Shortly after his triumph of pushing through the council's fair wages clause, Will was out walking down Commercial Road when he came across a small haggard looking woman sweeping up what looked like soot from in front of her house. "Mr. Crooks!" she exclaimed when she saw him approach. "God bless you for winning a place on the London Council. It's wonderful to know that we have one of our own on the council that actually understands us and the lives we have to live."

"Thank you, madam," said Will tipping his hat. "Is there anything you need help with?"

The woman indicated the black soot looking substance that she was sweeping up. "Can the council do anything to help us with the coal situation, Mr. Crooks? It's criminal the way the coal companies treat us. My Bert says there's no way those bags can hold the two hundredweight they are supposed to. Everybody knows the coal merchants are swindling us, Mr. Crooks and that we're not getting what we pay for. It's no wonder we're always running out of coal and so cold in the winter." Will was sympathetic. "I'm fully aware of the problem, madam, believe me. My family is just like most households in London that are being cheated by the coal merchants. As soon as I get myself onto the Control Committee, I'll get those people sorted out and I'll make sure by law that what they provide is what you've paid for. The coal merchants are just the type of company that has been fleecing off us Londoners for years."

It wasn't long at all before Will did get himself onto the Control Committee and he at once got to work by taking on the coal merchants. New rules were introduced that called for all bags of coal to meet the minimum size of two hundredweight. However, shortly after the new rules were introduced the committee received many letters of complaint accusing one merchant in particular of still delivering undersized goods while still charging the customers the full rate. When Will heard about this, he got the council's investigators to look into the matter further and found that it was indeed true. Will was outraged at this obvious snub of the new rules and contacted the merchant. He told the merchant that if he wanted to continue trading in London, not only would he need to provide the correct weight advertised, but that he would also need to pay damages to the customers that he had overcharged since the new rules were in place. With a clear cut choice of either no longer being able to legally trade in London, or pay damages, the unhappy merchant reluctantly agreed to pay the damages.

At the next Control Committee meeting, one of the older established council members raised the question, "Claiming damages and awarding such damages to the public, is this something that the council should be meddling in?"

Will stood and in response firmly said, "I say it is. If a man pays for something and doesn't get it and is too poor to take action himself, I say it is the duty of the public authority to see that he gets justice. And let me tell you gentleman that while I'm on this council and a member of this committee, I shall also do all in my power to not only make sure that weights of the coal are correct, but that the quality of that coal is not inferior to that being advertised on the ticket. I also intend to make sure that lamp oil is of good quality, and that people's rubbish bins are emptied regularly, and that the bakers bread is of proper weight, and that the milk comes from wholesome dairies and healthy cows, and that the coster in the street and the tradesman in the shop give good weight in everything they sell. I have been elected to this council on my promises to make better the lives of all Londoners, and I promise you gentlemen that I will."

23

Shortly after, Will entered the council building accompanied by John Burns. They chatted as they walked. Burns noticed a man in front of them carrying a very large leather briefcase. "Alexander!" he called. The man stopped and turned around and then smiled when he saw Burns. They exchanged greetings. "Alexander, this is my friend and fellow councilor, Will Crooks." Burns turned to Will. "Will, this is Alexander Binnie. He's our chief engineer and is working on the Blackwall Tunnel."

Will's face lit up as he thrust out his hand to shake Binnie's. "I'm so pleased to meet you!" Will said excitedly. "I've been pleading the case for a Thames crossing for the East End for years. We need to have free and easy access to the other side of the river. I cannot tell you how excited I am at this tunnel's construction." Binnie smiled broadly at Will's enthusiasm. "Well I'm pleased to meet somebody so enthusiastic about the project," he said.

"My word!" exclaimed Will. "It's going to be the longest underwater tunnel in the world and it's going to be right on my doorstep. Who wouldn't be enthusiastic about that? Just imagine the job opportunities that the tunnel will create for its neighbours and for future generations who'll be able to easily get from one side of the river to the other. Alexander, at some point could I see your plans for the project?"

"Certainly," said Binnie and he gave Will directions to his office. "Just pop along whenever you're free." They shook hands on it and said goodbye. As Binnie walked away, Burns laughed and said, "I thought you two would hit it off." Will grinned and patted Burns on his back as they walked towards their offices. "Thanks John!"

By the end of the day, Will had found time to visit Binnie. "Wow! You're eager!" laughed Binnie when Will knocked on his office door. "Come on in!"
Will's face lit up again when he saw all the plans and technical drawings that filled Binnie's office. "Here, look at these!" said Binnie as he led Will to a wall covered in plans of the tunnel.

"You're using the shield tunneling method, correct?" asked Will. Binnie looked surprised, and impressed. "Are you an engineer?" he asked seriously. Will laughed, "No, not at all, but I am fascinated by this. I've read about the shield tunneling because it was used on the Thames Tunnel. A Brunel invention I believe," he added as he studied the plans in front of him.

"Correct on both accounts," Binnie said happily. "Brunel said he was inspired by watching a creature called a shipworm, which is a mollusk. Brunel said he was fascinated at the efficiency of the shipworm when boring through submerged timber. Brunel witnessed this when he worked in a shipyard. This was Marc Isambard Brunel by the way and not his son Isambard Kingdom Brunel, although Isambard Kingdom also worked on the Thames Tunnel." He then added, "Also, along with the shield, we're using compressed air and cast iron rings. Unfortunately this job is also going to be a lot trickier than the Thames Tunnel."

"Why is that?" asked Will.

"Well to be begin with, unlike the Thames Tunnel, the river bed under the Blackwall Tunnel is composed of sand rather than clay; this is going to present some real difficulties. Also, at some points the tunnel will only be 5 feet, 6 inches below the bed of the river. We also need to make sure that the bottom of the tunnel is not more than 89 feet below the high water mark."

"Why is that?" asked Will.

"It's because it's important that there shouldn't be an air pressure of more than 35lb. per square inch," said Binnie.

"Of course," laughed Will. "I should have known that."

Binnie smiled and said, "We're going to divide the project into three separate sections; open approach roads with concreted-brick retaining walls; cut-and–cover sections lined with concrete and white glazed bricks; and then the cast iron tunnel; 1,220 feet of which will lay directly beneath the river."

"You know, Alexander," said Will excitedly. "I thought I was excited about the tunnel before I'd seen all of this, but now I can barely contain my excitement. Would it be possible to come down to the site with you for a close up look at the work going on there?"

"Why certainly, Will, but I can tell you what else you need to do for yourself and the project as a whole, and that is get yourself onto the bridges committee. Let me know if I can help in that respect."

"What a grand idea!" said Will and shortly after he did indeed become a member of the LCC bridges committee that was overseeing the construction of the tunnel.

Will thoroughly enjoyed his trip to see the work being carried out at the tunnel and had an endless stream of questions, not only for Binnie, but also for the regular workers on the project. When the bridges committee next met, Will relayed back to its members in excited and intricate detail the wonders of the engineering that he had witnessed.

The Chairman, Mr. Osborn said, "We've all been down to the site in our capacity of committee members, but I can honestly say that I've never heard the project explained with such passion and enthusiasm before. As momentous a project as this is, it is after all just a tunnel, and not a very exciting subject, however, the way that you have just relayed your visit to it and explained the latest developments, you've actually filled me with a desire to roll up my sleeves and get myself over to Blackwall to help with the digging." The other committee members around the table all laughed. "We have a few public meetings set up, Will, to keep the public updated and to continue to sell the project; after all, not everybody is in favour of such a large expensive project that far east. Will you be our representative at the meetings and give a speech on the tunnel?"

"Mr. Chairman, I would love to," Will said.

The meetings were such a success that the committee was soon receiving requests from all over London for Will to give his tunnel lecture. He made himself such an expert on the details of the tunnel that the chief engineers who heard his lecture congratulated him on how he made the project intelligible and interesting to the public. As usual, Will was 100 percent committed to his new role and tirelessly threw himself into touring London to give his tunnel lecture and to promote the project, while frequently visiting the site to keep up with the work and of course, the workers.

24

Will's reputation was growing fast and he was impressing a lot of people, and not just the poor and the working classes. One day while at the council building he looked up from his desk when he heard a knock on his office door, which was already ajar. His face lit up when he recognised his former manager from the Brewery that he had left to enter public life.

"Hello Bob," said Will as he jumped up and shook his hand vigorously. "How are you?"

"I'm doing good thanks, Will," he said happily. "I see that you're making quite a name for yourself already."

"Well I'm only doing my job," Will said modestly.

"Hmm, I think it's a bit more than just doing your job, Will, which is why I'm here."

"Well sit yourself down then, Bob and tell me what's on your mind," said Will as he pointed to the chair opposite his desk.

"There's a vacancy at the Brewery that we hope you'll be interested in. Now I know you're more than happy working here, Will, but this is a great opportunity."

"Go on then," said Will, so Bob continued.

"Not only is this a management position," said Bob, "but it may also eventually lead to a partnership offer for you. The pay is good too; £500 a year. I know you have six children to provide for. Just think of the future. Taking this job will set you and your family up for life. I also know about the Poplar Labour League's Will Crooks wages fund and that doesn't sound like very much security when you have six little ones to take care of."

"My word!" said Will, clearly moved. "That is indeed a great opportunity." For a moment he looked as though he was actually contemplating accepting the offer as he leaned back in his chair and looked deep in thought. At last he said, "I gave up the workshop for a life in public service because I want to serve the people. Making money is just not that important to me. Now what is important for me is the Labour movement. A manager, no matter how sympathetic, would not be able to remain in the Labour movement. So although I'm honoured to receive such an offer from you, I must decline."

"Really, Will? You choose to stay a working class man in public service living off a wages fund over the chance to be a partner in the Brewery and the monetary rewards that could come from that?"

"I do, Bob. I'm in a position to be one of the builders of a new London and bring in some long needed changes to our society. That is more important to me than any money."

Will's friend and fellow Labour activist, George Lansbury (Grandfather of the actress Angela Lansbury) who he had first met during the dock strike asked, "What's wrong?" when he saw a dejected looking Will.

"I was talking to a woman today who was absolutely terrified of going into the workhouse and who can blame the old dear. It's not right, George that working men who know what it's like to be poor cannot serve on the boards that administer the Poor Law."

"What are the current requirements for the Poplar Guardians Board?" asked Lansbury.

"There's a £40 property qualification," sighed Will.

"Well if anyone can get that changed, Will, it's you."

Will actually smiled at this. "Thanks George! You know, maybe I just will try to get it changed after all."

At the next meeting of the Poplar Trustees, of which Will was one, he persuaded the trustees to ask the Local Government Board to make it possible for working people to become Guardians. He was surprised when Mr. Richie, the President of the Government Board actually lowered the property qualification to £10. As great as this was, however, it still didn't help Will as he did not own any property. Will, as was his nature did not let the matter drop and with the backing of the other trustees he continued to write to the Local Government Board to try to get them to abolish the property qualification altogether. Will could hardly believe it when he received a reply in the mail one day telling him that Mr. Richie had been replaced as President of the Board by Sir Henry Fowler and that Sir Henry had decided to grant Will's request to abolish the property qualification altogether.

When the time came for the next election of the Poplar Guardians, both Will and Lansbury ran for places on the board and both were successfully elected; Will was even voted in at the top of the Poll due to his growing reputation in the area. He and Lansbury were the only two Labour men on the 24 man board; that same board where 30 years previously, he, along with his mother and siblings had stood in front of quivering in fear at being told that they should go to the workhouse.

When Will and Lansbury entered that very same room where Will had once stood all those years before to take their places on the board, Will stopped in the middle of the room in the exact spot where he had once stood clinging to his mother's skirt and for a moment he could not move as

Where there's a Will, there's a way

vivid visions from the past flooded over him. He felt a hand rest gently on his shoulder. "Are you all right, Will?" Lansbury asked. Will nodded. "Yes thanks, George. It just feels a little strange standing here again. Some memories are so etched into you that they are as clear as the day they actually happened."

"Yes indeed," agreed Lansbury, solemnly. "Especially the bad ones." When the other members of the board began entering the room, Will and Lansbury took their seats among them.

As the meeting progressed, Will stood and addressed the room and made it clear that he was not one to be messed with. "As a London County Councilor that has dealings on a daily basis with the ratepayers of Poplar, I can tell you that most are quite dissatisfied with the Board of Guardians. It has also come to my knowledge that the Local Government Board has evidence in its possession that the poor of the district are saying that if you want out-relief you must move into a street where rents are collected by someone who has influence with this board. Please be aware that myself and my friend here, Mr. Lansbury, will do all in our power to make sure that the board is run fairly and that out-relief will be given regardless of where a person resides, but will in fact be based as it should be on the person's circumstances."

As he let that bit of news sink in, he looked down at the large open book in front of him. Leafing through its pages and not looking up he said, "I see we keep a log of the dates that board members visit the workhouse. I assume updating this log is voluntary as I see there are two members of this board that have been Guardians for two years now, but there are no entries in the log at all to show that you have ever entered the workhouse." Now he did look up and in turn gave both Guardians in question searching looks. The first man held Will's gaze for a few seconds and looked as though he was going to say something before deciding otherwise and instead lowered his eyes and let them rest on his hands as he twiddled his thumbs hoping Will's gaze would move to the other Guardian that was also being singled out, which of course it did. The other man, however, did not shrink away from Will's questioning look. "There is nothing that says we have to actually visit the workhouse, even as a Guardian. I think we have a good understanding of such places even though we haven't been in one." replied the second Guardian defensively.

"Indeed," replied Will as he sat back down, clearly not impressed. "I think some changes are in order around here gentlemen."

The next day, Will decided to pay a visit to the workhouse himself. When he arrived at the workhouse gate he was met by a burly looking man who eyed him suspiciously. "State your business," he said coldly when he saw that Will wasn't dressed like the usual pauper's arriving at the gates.

"I'm Will Crooks, one of the Poplar Guardians and I would like to enter the workhouse in that capacity."

"It's not house committee day is it?" the man asked, sounding like he already knew the answer to that question.

"I beg your pardon," said Will, clearly confused.

"We only have Guardian visits on their regular committee visiting days," the gatekeeper told Will.

"In the past maybe, but I am a new Guardian and I would like to enter now, thank you!"

"I can't let you in if it's not committee day," the gatekeeper informed him. "Let me get the Master and see what he says." He left Will at the gate as he walked over to the entrance of the workhouse, occasionally looking back over his shoulder at Will as if trying to weigh him up. At last the workhouse Master appeared; followed closely by the gatekeeper.

"Can I help?" the Master asked. Will noticed that he did not sound the least bit helpful in spite of his offer.

"Yes! I'm Will Crooks and I'm one of the new Poplar Guardians. I'd like to come inside and take a look around please."

"It's not house committee day!" the Master said.

"So I've been told," said Will, quickly losing his patience. "But as a Guardian I demand entry today!"

"I think you'll find, Mr. Crooks that it's in the hands of the Master who gets in to visit and at this time I must tell you that it's not convenient."

"So be it!" said Will crossly, "But I promise you that will change!"

The next day, Sir Henry Fowler of the Local Government Board had two visitors; Will and Lansbury. He soon understood that they were not happy. Sir Henry confirmed that the Master was well within his rights not to allow a Guardian access if the visit was not on a house committee day.

"But that's preposterous!" raged Will.

Lansbury added his weight to the argument. "But how on earth are we to see what is actually going on inside if we can't get access when we need it?" Will took over. "I'm sure everything will just look fine and dandy on committee day when the Guardians are expected; not as though many actually seem to take the trouble to visit the place that is. We need to be able to come and go as we please to get an accurate picture of what's going on inside." Lansbury chimed in again. "You can bet your life if the Master didn't want to let Will in, then there's things going on in there that he didn't want him to see."

Where there's a Will, there's a way

"All right gentlemen," said Sir Henry. "I'll issue an order that will let any Guardian enter the workhouse on any day and at any reasonable hour."

Will made full use of the new order. He went straight back to the workhouse demanding access. When the Master saw the order from the Local Government Board he had no choice but to let Will enter. Inside, Will found the conditions revolting. The officers were downright hostile towards him, but he ignored them and went about his business as he pleased. Nearly everyone that he saw looked painfully thin, dirty and carried expressions of utter hopelessness on their wretched faces. Will found it heartbreaking. The clothes these poor people were wearing were not much better than filthy rags. Will stopped to talk to the inmates. The first person that he spoke to was an elderly man who began to cry as soon as he began to talk. Between sobs be blurted, "Poverty's no crime guvnor, but in here it's treated like it is."

Will noticed the old man cringe back slightly as another inmate passed close by. Will looked just in time to see the younger inmate passing by sneer at the older man. He looked a lot fitter and better fed than everyone Will had seen so far. "What was that all about?" asked Will. The old man looked ashamed as he said, "The younger, stronger men have the run of the place. The officers are too scared or just don't care enough to do anything about it. I did have a young nephew here that used to stand up for me, but he couldn't take it any longer so he deliberately kept breaking the rules and causing trouble. He knew he'd be sent to the magistrate and then be sent to prison instead. It's common for inmates here to try to get into prison. They say people are treated better there."

The next person Will stopped to talk to was an elderly woman who didn't even have any shoes on her feet; her clothing was filthy dirty too.

"What's your name?" Will asked gently.

"Mabel, sir," she said meekly.

"Is that all the clothing you have, madam?"

"Yes, sir!" she replied.

"Don't you have any footwear?"

"No, sir."

"If you have no other clothes, what happens when those are washed?" Will asked, pointing at the clothes she was wearing.

"We have to try and borrow from others any bits of clothing they can do without while ours go off to be washed." She lowered her voice as she added "We had all the bed linen returned by the laundry people, sir, because it was overrun by vermin and they wouldn't wash it."

The next time Will visited it was at meal time. Skilly, along with bread so tough it was likened to rubber was still the staple diet of the workhouse. As

Will walked along by the side of the wooden benches where the inmates ate, he noticed that they were picking little black things out of the skilly and throwing them aside. "Can I ask what you're doing?" Will asked one of the men eating.

"Yes guvnor, I'm picking out the rat droppings!" the man said calmly.

"My god!" cried Will, appalled.

"You!" he shouted at an officer nearby. "Where is the oatmeal stored for the skilly?" The officer did not respond.

"Well man?" shouted Will as a stunned silence filled the dining hall. "If you want to keep your job you'll answer me now!" Reluctantly the officer muttered, "In the oatmeal bin near the kitchen."

"Show me!" said Will angrily as he stood aside to let the officer lead the way. The officer stood his ground for a while before deciding to do as he was told. "This way!" he spat and glared at Will as he stepped in front of him and led him to the oatmeal bin. When Will opened the door of the bin the sight made him gag. Rats had free run of the place. It was obvious that no attempt was being made to stop the infestation or cleanse the oatmeal before it was prepared for the inmates to eat. With a heavy heart, Will trudged back to the dining hall struggling to believe the horrors that these poor people were living in just because they were poor. When he reached the dining hall he saw firsthand the stronger men fighting for anything that was edible from the weaker ones. "Aren't you going to do anything?" Will asked one of the officers. "No fear, I'll just get beaten too. I've already been threatened with murder. If it gets really out of hand then we'll call the police in, but if they're prosecuted then they'll only be sent to prison and prison holds no fear for them after being in here."

The next time Will saw Mabel she was distraught. "What on earth's wrong, Mabel?" Will asked.

"Oh sir, my friend Lily died last night in my arms. I tried to tell them how ill she was and that she needed help, but they just wouldn't listen to me. I begged them to help, but they weren't interested. They just don't care about us!" she wailed.

"Please come with me Mabel. I want you to show me which officers ignored you."

"I can't do that," she cried. "They'll make my life hell if I do that."

"No they won't!" said Will. "I can guarantee that."

"Are you sure?" she asked.

"Oh I'm sure!" Will reassured her.

Hesitantly, Mabel pointed out the officers to him. "I want to know why you didn't do anything for the poor old lady that died last night?" Will demanded of the officers.

"We didn't think she was ill," one of them replied.
"Yeah, they're always pulling stuff like that," the other added.
"So you're both medically trained are you?" Will asked.
"No," they both replied.
"So you had no way of knowing if she was really ill or not?"
They didn't answer the question but just shrugged. "Besides, we were too busy to help."
"Busy with what?" Will wanted to know.
Again they shrugged. "Don't remember now."
"It sounds to me that you don't particularly care what happened to the old lady and she was just a bit of an inconvenience." Again they just shrugged.
"As a Guardian I have the power to suspend you both, so please get your things and leave the building. I'll be recommending to the board that you're dismissed."

The board did indeed dismiss the officers and they were not the last either. With the help of Lansbury, Will saw to it that the officers and the Guardians that had no desire to treat the poor with respect and kindness were weeded out and replaced with a more intelligent and more sympathetic staff. Will also saw to it that inmates were nursed better and clothed better; the old workhouse clothing was replaced by simple, homely garments.

From his own memories of the workhouse, he could not forget the awful taste of skilly, or the gagging he endured while trying to swallow it, so he set out to improve the inmate's food as well. The bread that was being supplied by contract from outside was the first thing to go. He developed a system for bread making in the workhouse itself. He brought in a couple of skilled bakers to teach and oversee the workhouse bread making system. They soon made all the bread that was required in the workhouse for the inmates, the officers, the children's schools and all the loaves that were given as out-relief to the poor. The bread was so good in fact that the Daily Mail newspaper described it as being equal to that which could be obtained in the best restaurants in the West End of London. Yet they were making the bread cheaper in the workhouse than for what it was possible to buy bread on the outside for. The work also provided many of the inmates with a pleasant and useful occupation.

Will then went a step further and got the board to replace margarine with butter, gave the inmates fresh meat, got them milk that had not been skimmed and got them unadulterated tea and coffee. He even went as far as getting the older women in the workhouse sugar for their tea and coffee, and even let the older men smoke an occasional pipe of tobacco.

News of these improvements, however, soon reached the ears of the austere Local Government Board, so it sent down its inspectors to Poplar to investigate. The inspectors were then quickly followed by the President of the Board himself, Mr. Henry Chaplin, who had since taken over from Sir Henry Fowler. After Mr. Chaplin's visit, he sent a letter of his findings to the Guardians. Not only was he happy and impressed by what he saw in Poplar, but he issued a circular to Guardians all across the country recommending to them all that Poplar had introduced. He even proposed that for deserving old folk over 64 years of age that the supply of tobacco, dry tea and sugar be made compulsory and the new dietary scale should be introduced everywhere. However, instead of other boards welcoming this improved treatment of the workhouse poor, a revolt materialised and a deputation of Guardians went to Whitehall to try to persuade the President of the Board into a rethink. Will and Lansbury also attended the meeting to defend the new system.

By the time the meeting took place, Mr. Chaplin was no longer President, but had been succeeded by Mr. Walter Long. The Guardians, one by one, explained that it wasn't that they didn't want the best for the poor, but it was a matter of cost and of the extra book-keeping involved that they were against the new system.

As Guardian after Guardian repeated the same thing, Mr. Long at last interrupted the proceedings. "Gentlemen, am I to understand that you do not desire to feed your poor people properly then? If those are the best reasons you can give me for not introducing the new system to your workhouses then your arguments have failed." From that day forth, the changes, including the new dietary scale were introduced throughout the entire workhouse system of the land. Will had not only improved the lives of all the unfortunate poor people in the workhouse in Poplar, but his actions had now improved the lives of the poor in workhouses all over the country too.

26

Will's work at changing the face of London and promoting the Labour movement was a rewarding one, but also a time consuming one. When he did return home at night it was to a home being run more and more by his children; his eldest daughter, Minnie, now 18, leading the way as his wife Tilly's health continued to decline.

Before the first year of his public service was out, Will was interrupted one day at his LCC office at Spring Gardens by a uniformed messenger boy who handed him a telegram. It was from Minnie and read, "You need to come home now. Mother has taken a turn for the worse. The Doctor said to send for you."

Will rushed home as fast he could to find the Doctor and his eldest children in the bedroom with Tilly. The curtains were drawn and only a small lamp illuminated the room. Minnie sat on the side of the bed next to her mother holding her hand, but moved aside to let Will take her place. Tilly was barely conscious as he took her hand in his. When he looked at the Doctor, the Doctor simply shook his head; there was nothing that could be done. Will swallowed deeply and fought back his tears. "Oh Tilly, I'm so sorry. I should have spent more time here at home with you."

She managed to turn her head slightly in Will's direction and in little more than a whisper, said, "Nonsense Will, your work is too important."

Will kissed the back of her hand gently and said, "I love you so much Tilly." At hearing this she closed her eyes and smiled weakly. Will then sat in silence and held her hand waiting for the end to come. The only sound in the room came from the large clock that sat on the mantelpiece as it loudly counted down the last minutes of Tilly's life. Soon her hand fell lifeless in his. His beloved Tilly was dead. Consumed in grief, he was oblivious to the clock's mockery of the dead as it ticked on relentlessly, reminding us all that time marches on, with or without us.

Will was now 40 years old and a widower with six children to raise; the youngest of which was still only two years old. It would appear his family commitments would have to cut short his promising career in public service.

Remarkably with the help of his eldest children, especially Minnie and his now aging mother, he managed to juggle his public duties with his home duties and quickly learned to be both father and mother to his children. When he returned home at night after a long day at work, or from addressing a Labour or Union meeting with the cheers still ringing in his ears, he would immediately jump in to help out with the children and the housework.

He had lots of issues that he wanted to address both at LCC and at Poplar Guardian level and he was soon back with the bit between his teeth. It was during a meeting of the Poplar Guardians that Will asked, "How many children do we have in our Poor Law school in Forest Gate?" The Chairman of the Board replied, "I don't have the exact figure to hand, but we usually have between 500 and 600 children living there."

"It's not ideal having the school so far away from us is it?" Will said thoughtfully. "That must be what, 4 or 5 miles away from us? Please correct me if I'm wrong, but my understanding is that if a child's parents are long standing regular inmates of the workhouse then the child in question gets to stay at the Forest Gate school, but my concern here is the 'ins and outs', the children of the parents that only come into the workhouse for short periods. Again my understanding is that we can send the child to the Forest Gate School, but that their parents can call them back the very next day when they leave the workhouse, even though we know the parents will probably be back in the house again soon after leaving."

"You understand the situation correctly, Mr. Crooks," the Chairman told him. "I'm afraid it's a problem that we haven't been able to solve as yet." Will looked concerned. "If the children are not getting a proper schooling and everything they do learn is how to be a pauper on the street or from inside the workhouse, then the only training that child is getting is for a life in pauperism. That just won't do! We must find a solution." Lansbury spoke, "Do you have any ideas?" he asked Will.

"Maybe," Will replied. He turned to the Chairman. "Mr. Chairman, I propose that we send these children to the regular surrounding public schools."

"What!" exclaimed the Chairman, along with a few other surprised Guardians. "Pauper children mixing with regular children in a public school? I can't see that suggestion going down well with the School Board. Besides, you know what children are like, the workhouse children will stand out like a sore thumb and will be teased relentlessly for being paupers."

"That part is easy enough to fix," said Will. "We can simply provide them with non-institution clothing so that they won't stand out as paupers." The Chairman was still not convinced. "I still can't see the School Board allowing it," he said.

"Have the Guardians ever asked them before?" asked Will.

"Well, no," admitted the Chairman.

"Do I have the Guardians backing to write to the London School Board to ask them?"

"Well yes, I suppose," said the Chairman. "But I really don't think they will entertain the idea."

"Thank you!" said Will, ignoring the Chairman's negative comments.

"I'll send them a letter."

At the next meeting of the board, Will raised the subject again. "I received a reply from the London School Board," he told the gathered Guardians. "Mr. Chairman, it appears that you were correct. The School Board do not seem willing to be helpful in this matter and list all manner of reasons why they think it would not work, however, after all of their objections they do finish off by saying that all the surrounding schools are nearly all full anyway and that if we can find any vacant places then we may send some of the children."

"Are you going to try and find these vacant places?" the Chairman asked. "It sounds like it may be a time consuming task."

"No!" said Will.

"Really?" asked Lansbury, surprised.

Will smiled at his friend. "They are the School Board. I am going to write back and tell them that as such it is their duty to find places for these and all children in the area. I'm also going to let them know that the Guardians are determined to see all of these children in day schools and that we won't back off until the School Board has found places for them all."

It wasn't long after that, that Will informed the Guardians that places had been found for all of the children, but Will still wasn't content. He was happy of course that these children now got to go to school like regular non pauper children and wore clothes that helped them fit in, but it concerned him that after a day at school getting an education, these poor children would have to return to the workhouse. He knew that these children would still grow up with the mark of the workhouse and pauperism upon them. Used to living as they were in the workhouse, these children would often grow up bearing the stamp of the workhouse on them into adulthood and thus primed and readied for an adult life in and out of the house. Will knew that to end this type of cycle, he needed to take the children out of the workhouse completely.

When the latest meeting of the Poplar Guardians came to order, Will stood and passed around the table some plans and drawings of a building.
"What are these?" asked the Chairman.
"These Mr. Chairman and fellow Guardians are the plans and drawings for a large dwelling house, which lies about a quarter of a mile away from the workhouse. I want us to purchase it!"
"What?" gasped the Chairman, echoed by quite a few of the other Guardians. "What on earth for?"
"I want this to be a safe house for the children that we set up in the regular schools," he told them. "So long as the mark of the workhouse clings to the children, so long will the children cling to the workhouse. Instead of after a successful day at school and heading back to the workhouse, I want those children housed here, away from the bad habits and horrors they witness there. I want to remove as much of the workhouse as we can from their lives. We need to act now to sever any links to the workhouse. Let's educate them as ordinary working class children so that they'll feel like ordinary working class children. That way they'll grow up into normal working class men and women so that as adults they'll no longer have to rely on the poor law, but the only way that we can do this is to remove them completely from the workhouse system. This is why we need to purchase this building!" After their initial shock at the idea had passed, the board agreed that it was indeed a very good idea and agreed to purchase the building.

28

1893

At home, Will's mother helped out with the children as best she could, but without a mother, and a father that was busily involved in his public duties, the children were becoming more and more of a handful. Because of her own infirmities, Will's mother found it easier to sometimes look after some of the younger children at her own small home in the High Street.

On his way home at the end of the day, Will would stop by to pick up his children, or if it was too late, just kiss them goodnight as they slept. His mother did not live alone; she had taken in a lodger, a nurse named Elizabeth Lake. Elizabeth had moved to London from Gloucester and Will had taken a liking to her immediately. She had a happy, easy going disposition and her loving and humanitarian nature sat well with her occupation as a nurse. Will's frequent visits to his mother's house meant that he and Elizabeth began to see rather a lot of each other. She loved having the children around and enjoyed helping out whenever she could, even though the children often got out of hand.

It soon became apparent to Will's mother that Elizabeth and Will got along together very well. Whenever Will visited and Elizabeth was at home, she would always want him to tell her in great detail about his latest dealings at the LCC and as a Guardian. One evening when Will arrived late at his mother's house, he found that the children were already in bed. After he had crept into the bedroom and kissed them goodnight he joined his mother and Elizabeth in the sitting room.

"Would you both like some tea?" Elizabeth asked. "Yes please," said Will.

"Oh not for me thanks, love," said Will's mother. "I'm exhausted." She faked a yawn. "I'm going to take myself off for an early night. Those children have worn me out today." While his mother took herself off to bed, Elizabeth got to work making the tea. When she had finished, she and Will sat talking deep into the night.

As the night drew on, Will couldn't stop himself from yawning. He was having a wonderful time, but tiredness was creeping up. "Oh I'm sorry, Will, I'm keeping you up," Elizabeth said.

"I'm the one that's sorry," said Will. "I'm having a lovely time, but it's just been another long and busy day."

Elizabeth smiled sympathetically. "I know it has, and I swear I don't know how you've managed to cope this past year with working as hard as you have and then having to look after your family too. What you need is a good capable wife to look after you and the children. Mind you, it's not every woman that'll face it. To start married life with a husband and six children is enough to make any woman think twice, and then twice again."

Will shifted uncomfortably in his chair. "Well I've been thinking the same thing myself. I know it's going to take somebody very special to take on me and six children and I don't mind telling you that I have my eye on the very woman for the job." Elizabeth looked pleased. "Well then, if I were you I'd lose no time in telling her so." Will looked embarrassed as he told her, "It's you!" Elizabeth's eyes widened in surprise. "Never!" she said. "I've been married once before and that's enough for one lifetime. No, Will, I couldn't face it! My first marriage was far from happy! When my husband died I promised myself I would never marry again. Plus the thought of being responsible for six children is just too daunting for me! No, Will, I just can't do it."

Will was sad, but it was no more than he had expected. "Will you at least think it over? I can't think of anyone else more suited."

Elizabeth did think it over; she knew that Will had been a kind husband to his first wife, was a good son to his mother and was widely known and respected in Poplar. If it wasn't for the six children he would be a good catch. The next time Will saw her he asked if she had reconsidered. Her answer was still no. Will was not easily deterred and the next time he saw her he again asked her if she had reconsidered, but still she said no, although she was beginning to enjoy the attention. She could also see that the situation with the family was not getting any easier. With no full time parental supervision the children were becoming even more unruly and there was a real threat of the family being broken up. This troubled Elizabeth.

As Will entered his mother's house one evening after another long day at the LCC, Elizabeth came out into the hall to greet him. He smiled and went to say hello, but before he could utter a word she said, "Will you promise me one thing?" He looked surprised at the abruptness of the question, but quickly recovered and said, "I'll promise you anything if you'll be my wife."

"The minute I marry you I'll be a stepmother and you know the bad name that stepmothers get. Nobody knows better than you do that the children are out of hand. I shall have to get their obedience before I can win their love, for if they don't respect me, they'd never love me. I may have to punish them."

"Well of course!" he agreed.

"Yes, it's of course now, but will it always be so? Will you trust me to be just, as well as kind? Will you hear the why and wherefore before you judge?"

"Elizabeth, please believe me when I say yes. I promise."

"Very well then," she said. "I accept your proposal!"

29

On March 30th, 1896, two bargemen were steering their cargo laden barges up the river Thames at Reading, when a lighter and faster sailing barge with its sails full got a little too close to the cargo barges, causing enough of a wash from its wake to push them closer to the river's bank. The bargemen while cursing the sailing barge, quickly grabbed their long barge poles and plunged them down into the murky river to stop their barges from being pushed even closer to the muddy bank.

"Hey, what's that, Albert?" one of the men cried, pointing down into the water. The other man looked down to see a tattered brown parcel bobbing up and down in the water as it lapped against the side of the barge. Quick as a flash he grabbed a long boat hook and swept up the package before the barge passed it by and placed it down on the barge floor. As soon as the barges were secure, the men went to the package to investigate. It was covered in thick, soggy brown wrapping paper and as soon as they touched it, one of the corners fell away revealing a tiny human leg.

"Oh my god!" cried the younger of the two men, visibly shaken. The older bargeman, who up until then had thought he had seen pretty much everything on the river, bent down and removed the rest of the brown paper. His heart sank. This time the young man by his side could only offer a groan of despair; neither of them could find words as the body of a baby girl lay before them; white edging tape had been wrapped around her neck. She had been strangled.

When the police arrived on the scene they immediately began to drag the river. They hoped that this was just a one-off killing, a poor helpless victim of one of the darker aspects of Victorian life; 'Baby Farming'. Baby farmers acted as adoption or fostering agents and were in the business of taking in unwanted babies, and in return for a fee, taking care of them, which usually meant letting them die or killing them. The main goal of a baby farmer was to come by as many sickly infants as they could, because life hung in the balance for them and their deaths would appear more natural and so not be investigated. The infants were then practically starved and kept drugged on laudanum, paregoric, and other poisons. Godfrey's Cordial, which contained opium and was also known as 'Mother's Friend' was often used to quieten the babies as they slowly died.

The majority of baby farmers were women, and they placed their advertisements in most of the newspapers which catered to working class girls; looking especially for mothers with illegitimate babies who were struggling to find work while also trying to care for a baby; let alone struggling to deal with the social stigma of their situation. A typical advertisement would read:

'WANTED: Child to adopt.
Childless couple would like to adopt a young infant to raise as our own. If weak or in poor health would receive a parent's loving care. Terms, 12 Shillings a month; or would adopt entirely for the small sum of £10.00.'

Meanwhile, as the river was being dragged, a young woman by the name of Evelina Marmon sat in her small, simply furnished room at the boarding house in Cheltenham where she currently resided waiting for her visitor. As she waited, she gently rocked her baby daughter, Doris, in her arms and softly sung her a lullaby; the same lullaby that her own mother had sung to her 25 years previously when she herself was brought into the world on her parents farm. The farm girl, however, had grown up and become bored of life on the farm and had decided to move to the city for a more exciting life. With her blonde hair, buxom figure and friendly manner, she soon found employment at the Plough Hotel, an old coaching inn where she became popular with the customers; so popular in fact that she quickly found herself pregnant. The father of the child had deserted her and left her to her own devices, so now she sat in her room; her beautiful baby in her arms and waited for her visitor to arrive.

Alone and unmarried, Evelina knew it would be almost impossible for her to keep the baby. The shame that unmarried mothers carried with them in Victorian times she could have lived with, but there was just no way that she could work and also care for a child. She decided that she would 'adopt out' little Doris as many unmarried mothers in her position were forced to do. She hoped to find someone that would take on Doris for a weekly fee so that she could go back to work and if things worked out well for her in the future then she would hopefully be able to reclaim her daughter. She had therefore placed an advertisement in the miscellaneous section of the Bristol Times and Mirror newspaper; it read: "Wanted, respectable woman to take young child." When the newspaper came out and she read her own advertisement, she noticed that right next to it another advertisement had been placed; it read:

'Married couple with no family would adopt healthy child, nice country home. Terms, £10.'

Evelina couldn't believe her luck; the couple in the advertisement seemed perfect. She answered the advertisement and promptly received a reply from a Mrs. Harding in Reading, who wrote, "I should be glad to have a dear little baby girl, one I could bring up and call my own. We are plain, homely people, in fairly good circumstances. I don't want a child for money's sake, but for company and home comfort. Myself and my husband are dearly fond of children. I have no child of my own. A child with me will have a good home and a mother's love. Rest assured I will do my duty by that dear child. I will be a mother, as far as lies in my power. It is just lovely here, healthy and pleasant. There is an orchard opposite our front door."

It was more than Evelina could ever have dreamed of for Doris, but try as she might to persuade Mrs. Harding to take a weekly fee, still clinging to the hope that one day in the future she could take Doris back, Mrs. Harding would not budge. She was resolute in her demands for a full adoption and a one-off payment in advance of £10.00. Although this wasn't what Evelina wanted, she reluctantly agreed, for she knew that Doris would have a good life with the Harding's.

Evelina now sat in her small room with a heavy heart waiting for the arrival of Mrs. Harding. When she arrived, Evelina was surprised that Mrs. Harding was a lot older than she had expected, well into her 50's in fact, but she had arrived with a warm shawl to wrap baby Doris in to protect her from the outside cold, and when Evelina saw the way Mrs. Harding fussed over Doris she couldn't help but think that a full adoption would indeed be best for Doris, and so she handed over the £10.00.

Evelina then accompanied Mrs. Harding and Doris to Cheltenham station and then boarded the train with them. She stayed with them until Gloucester. When she stood to leave them, she wept uncontrollably at the thought of leaving Doris. "Don't fret my dear," Mrs. Harding said kindly, trying to comfort her as she swaddled Doris. "We'll be home in Reading soon, the start of her new life. The house will be nice and cosy when we get there. She'll be fine. I'll write and keep you up to date too. I promise." Evelina reluctantly said goodbye to her baby daughter, and sobbing, left the train.

When the train reached Reading, however, Mrs. Harding made no attempt to get off. In fact, at 9 p.m. when the train pulled into Paddington Station in London, she was still on board. When she left the train at Paddington, she took an omnibus to Willesden in North London and got off at Mayo Road. As soon as she entered her rented rooms, she took some white edging tape and wrapped it around Doris's tiny neck and then pulled it tight and watched the poor helpless child as it struggled for its last breath. Mrs. Harding was in reality a woman named, Amelia Dyer.

Incredibly, the next day, another baby, 13 month old Harry Simmons was also brought home by Dyer, along with another payment of £10.00. Sadly, he was to quickly follow baby Doris's fate.

The next evening, Dyer placed both dead babies into her carpet bag, along with some bricks (to weigh the bag down) and took the train to Reading. Once there she found a quiet spot that she had used before by Caversham Lock and then forced the carpet bag through the railings and waited for the splash as it hit the cold water of the Thames below, where it then sank out of sight to the bottom of the river.

Back at the site where the bargemen had found the baby's body, the Reading Borough Police officers that were investigating the death couldn't quite believe their luck. The brown wrapping paper that had been wrapped around the dead child was still in remarkably good condition; so much so that the police could see a railway label attached to it from Temple Meads station in Bristol and on the label they were able to make out the faint outline of a name, Mrs. Thomas, and an address. Mrs. Thomas was in fact another alias for the afore mentioned killer of baby Doris, Amelia Dyer.

A few days after the dead baby in the river had been found, police raided the address on the label. Although the police officers reeled from the stench of human decomposition as they entered the house, they found no other dead bodies. What they did find, however, was the tell-tale white edging tape that was used on the victim pulled from the river by the bargemen, along with telegrams arranging adoptions, receipts from baby farming type advertisements and many letters from mothers asking about their young ones. From the information that they found there, the police could see that as least 20 children had been placed with Dyer.

There was a public outcry when the details of Dyer's atrocities were released. Will, now Chairman of the Public Control Committee on the LCC was outraged too. The Infant Life Protection Act of 1872 had failed miserably in protecting the lives and well-being of the infants it was set up to protect, even though as early as 1873 the Metropolitan Board of Works, which was responsible for implementing the Act, informed the then Home Secretary that evasion of the Act was rampant, but sadly appropriate action was not taken to rectify the situation.

So Will and the Public Control Committee on behalf of the LCC pushed for an Amendment to that Act. They wanted stricter new powers for local authorities to actively seek out baby farms and lying-in houses and also to be able to enter homes suspected of abusing children, and to then remove those children to a place of safety. They also pushed for any person or body that cared for more than one child to be registered with the local authority.

On May 5th, Will, as Chairman of the Public Control Committee represented the LCC at the Houses of Parliament where a Select

Committee led by the Chairman, the Earl of Denbigh, sat to consider the amendment to the Infant Life Protection Act. Will was questioned at length. During his questioning, the Earl of Denbigh asked him, "Mr. Crooks, you say that you are in favour of extending the Act; is it your opinion that registration would be advantageous?"

"I am positively sure of it," Will responded.

The Earl of Denbigh: "Do you think that the feelings of the working classes, as a general rule, those whom you have come into contact with, are generally in favour of the proposals of this Bill?"

Will: "Most decidedly."

The Earl of Denbigh: "Instances have been brought before the Committee of cases of possible hardship if an extended system of registration were in force; can you give us any instances of the general practice of working men with reference to their children when they have not got a mother to look after them, and when the men themselves have to go away from home in search of work?"

Will: "Yes. I can give you many."

The Earl of Denbigh: "Can you tell the committee what they generally do?"

Will: "A man who is left with a family of children, or a man whose wife has deserted him, finds always considerable difficulty in placing those children in good homes, and invariably men who find themselves in that dilemma in my immediate neighbourhood come to me. They say,

"Can't you get the Guardians to take my children?" and I say, "I really cannot; the law is against it unless you personally go into the workhouse with the children," and they say, "Well what do you advise that I shall do?" I say, "Have you no sister-in-law, no mother-in-law, no relation whatever that you can place the children with?"

"No."

"Do you think that you could afford to keep a woman to look after your children?"

"Well I think I could if I could find a proper woman to do it." I then make a suggestion of this sort: "Now what I want to say to you is, that you had better go and look round and find some decent people who have a couple of rooms to let in their house, take the rooms, state the whole of the circumstances of the case to the landlady, say to her that you have a daughter or a son, 9, 10, or 12 years of age, as the case might be, and generally they can look after the little ones, and that if the landlady will give an eye to them you will make it worth her while." The particular case that I have in my mind must have been very successful indeed; for last week, in going through a thoroughfare, a man rushed up to me, shook me by the hand, and said, "I am so glad to see you, Mr. Crooks; I took your advice." I did not quite understand what the man meant, and he said, "Don't you remember that I came to your house and asked you about my children?" I said, "No, there are so many men who come to me that I do not remember this particular instance." He said, "Well I have taken two rooms in such-and-such a street, and the children are going on well, and I assure you that I shall never pass you again as long as I live," meaning that he would give me some kind of acknowledgment for the advice given to him.

The other instance I have in my mind is the case of a man who came to the Guardians with two babies; roughly speaking one must have been about two years old, a diminutive little thing, and the other about six months; and in a most imploring manner he asked the Guardians to take the children. The Guardians said, "We cannot take the children without you. Where is your wife?"

"My wife has gone to a hospital very bad. I cannot go to work. I have these two babies to look after, and I can't get no one to take them, or at least, no person respectable enough, and sober enough, to look after my children in the way that I should like." The man was in a terrible way. I was so struck with him that I followed him out across the road and got into conversation with him, and I said, "Now what do you propose to do?"

"What can I do? I shall starve if I go on like this; I cannot leave the children and I cannot get anyone whom I can trust the children with."

"Very well," I said, "Now look here; you go back to the relieving officer; you see the children are gradually getting worse; they certainly could not have been left like that when their mother went away; you go and ask the relieving officer to give you an order and then go into the workhouse with the children, and tomorrow I will come and see you, and perhaps I shall think of some better plan by which I can get your children placed out than I can think of today, or I may find some institution that would look after the children."

The Earl of Denbigh: "But what we really want to know is this: you put the children out, you found a lodging for these children?"

Will: "No, we did not. The man went away and did not go into the workhouse with the children. The point I want to make there is that if houses were registered, or if this man knew perfectly well that any person that took his children would be under inspection and registered, there would be a safeguard at once, and it would encourage him to find a decent person to take his children to; he would have said to himself, "You must register; the inspector will be sufficient guarantee for me that these children are being properly looked after." Now, without that registration and without that power of inspection the man had no guarantee that his youngsters would be properly looked after at all."

The Earl of Denbigh: "Can you give us any experience of the working of what is called the adoption system; that is, giving out the children on the payment of a lump sum down?"

Will: "I can only give this experience: that we get into the workhouse several children who have either been adopted for a lump sum down or taken on a promise of a weekly payment which has ceased, and in regard to whom we get, there is absolutely no guarantee that the children are illegitimate, have been boarded out or have been adopted. The foster mother or father comes up and says, "I have a little girl or a boy that has been left with me under promise of payment, and I have not seen the mother or the father for a year, or for three months, as the case may be, and I cannot afford to keep it; and the Guardians must take it." so the Guardians are obliged to take it."

The Earl of Denbigh: "You regard it as generally a very bad thing for the child, I suppose, that a lump sum should be paid down with it?"

Will: "I do indeed!"

The Earl of Denbigh: "Can you suggest any method of preventing children being given out on the payment of a lump sum?"

Will: "I think that the amended Act should be framed to make it a penal offence to accept a lump sum, with a child of that description."

The Earl of Denbigh: "Were you going to give me some other reasons for supporting the Bill?"

Will: "Yes. My other reasons are these. I am acquainted with a lady who does, and has done, a tremendous lot of rescue work, and she has passed through her hands in the 18 or 20 years she has been engaged in the occupation of rescue work, no fewer than 3000 young women. At the present moment she has lying in her house five young women recently confined. She says that, speaking for herself, she should be delighted if her house could be registered, and that the inspector might go from time to time to the children she places out. She boards them out, one only in a house; she pays 5 shillings a week for the children until the mother can afford to pay; she secures a situation for the mother; and she is induced to do this by the fact that where the child can be kept alive and looked after, the mother is encouraged to become a respectable young woman and is encouraged to work and toil for the child, which keeps her from going into bad ways. In supporting this amendment herself, she says, "I believe that people with whom I place the children would be very glad indeed to be registered; and what is more, if they were not glad to be registered I should object to their having the children at all, for I should say at once it was not a desirable home; for in every instance the greatest amount of publicity should be given to these cases; that is to say, those who have the care and study of these children."

Lord Thring, also on the committee interrupted: "Mr. Crooks, do you think that people like being called baby farmers?"

Will: "A certified house would not be called a baby farm for any long time to come."

Lord Thring: "But at the present time they call them baby farmers?"

Will: "You do not call a person in the country who accepts children to board out, a baby farmer."

Lord Thring: "I ask you is not that the common term used; if a person is registered, we call him or her a baby farmer?"

Will: "No, the working classes are not so rude as is generally suggested."

Lord Thring: "You have told us broadly that the working people are in favour of registration; I want to know what possible evidence you have that the working men in Poplar are in favour of registration?"

Will: "I think I have the best of all reasons for saying that. I am in daily contact with the men to begin with. I address in my own neighbourhood on an average three public meetings a week. I have taken the subject of this Bill three or four times since we began to talk about the framing of the Bill, and on every occasion the Bill has been squarely debated by the men assembled at the meeting, and a resolution has been carried in favour of supporting the Bill. I cannot go any further than that."

Viscount Llandaff, another committee member: "The chief object of this amended Bill would be for the benefit of the houses, as far as I can make out; a certificate of goodness?"

Will: "Yes."

Lord Kinnaird, another member of the committee: "You distinctly think that there are many children who are not treated as well as they ought to be, whose treatment would be improved? There is sufficient cause made out for extending the Act, you think?"

Will: "I do think so; I think it would encourage even the indifferent ones, ones which would not be inclined now to register as good homes to improve. When those people were desirous of taking in children, they would put their house in order; and though you might have to strike them off the register for one year, you might put them on the next if they showed the necessary improvement."

On May 22nd, Amelia Dyer appeared at the Old Bailey and pleaded guilty to the murder of Doris Marmon, but she also pleaded insanity as she had twice been committed to mental asylums in Bristol. The prosecution, however, argued successfully that her bouts of mental instability had been a ploy to avoid suspicion as both committals were said to have coincided with times when Dyer was worried that her crimes might have been exposed. It took the jury just four and a half minutes to find her guilty.

June 10th, 1896

Amelia Dyer was hanged by James Billington at Newgate Prison at 9 a.m. precisely. He was paid £10.00 for the job, which was the going rate, although the cost of rail travel to Newgate was also reimbursed. This ex-Sunday school teacher when not engaged in executions ran a barber shop in Farnworth. He was responsible for the execution of 24 men and three women in his time as Executioner for the City of London and Middlesex. It was a job that he enjoyed immensely as one who had had a life long obsession with hanging. He even made replica gallows in his back garden on which he practiced with weights and dummies. Throughout his career, Billington executed 150 men and women.

At 57, Dyer was the oldest woman to go to the gallows in more than 50 years. It's uncertain just how many infants Amelia Dyer actually murdered, but estimates range from 50 to over 400 during her 15 to 20 year murderous spree. Moving homes around the country frequently helped her to avoid detection for so long. Her ghost was said to haunt Newgate Prison.

At the House of Commons, Will spent many a day in the Commons Committee Room working with and arguing with barristers and Members of Parliament to protect innocent infants from cruelty and neglect. His hard work prevailed. The Bill was passed and became 'The Infant Life Protection Act.'

The Act, which came into effect the following year, required that all persons retaining or receiving two or more infants under the age of five years for hire or reward and maintaining them apart from their parents for a longer period than 48 consecutive hours, must give notice to the County Council. The Council is then required to fix the number of infants which may be kept in a house as to which such notice has been given. Notice has also to be given to the Council when any infant under two years of age is taken for a lump sum not exceeding £20. The Council is empowered to remove a child from a house as to which notice has been given, when such child is found to be improperly kept, and in such case, or in the case of a person convicted under the Prevention of Cruelty to Children Act, that the person may not receive any more infants except with the consent of the Council in writing. No infant could be kept in a home that was so unfit and so overcrowded as to endanger its health, and no infant could be kept by an unfit care giver who threatened, by neglect or abuse, its proper care and maintenance.

Two male inspectors and three women inspectors were appointed by the LCC to carry out the provisions of the Act. Persons guilty of an offence against the Act were liable to a penalty not exceeding £5 or to imprisonment for not more than six months, and any fines were to be paid to the council.

The Act finally gave real power to local authorities to control the adoption and lying-in business. Will had succeeded in dealing a major blow against baby farming in London.

1896

As a nine year old boy, Will had spent three weeks in the workhouse before being moved on to the Poor Law school in Sutton. 35 years later across London in Walworth, another young boy aged just seven had also just entered the workhouse where he too would spend three weeks before being moved on to a Poor Law school.

The boy was the son of two music hall performers that had separated before he was even two years old. Deserted by his alcoholic father, his mother, plagued as she was by ill health, could not keep the boy from entering the Newington workhouse. The boy's childhood was an endless struggle. When his mother was committed to a mental hospital, he was left to fend for himself on the tough streets of London.

It is little wonder, therefore, that the boy, touched as he was by poverty, as an adult would be able to bring that experience to bear when he gave the world its most beloved down-and-out; 'The Tramp'. The boy's name was Charlie Chaplin.

May 22nd, 1897

William Bull, the current chairman of the Bridges Committee was responsible for the arrangements for the official opening of the Blackwall Tunnel. On behalf of her majesty Queen Victoria, her son, his Royal Highness the Prince of Wales (the future King Edward VII) and the Princess of Wales (the future Queen Alexandra) traveled to Poplar to open the tunnel. Union Jacks flew from the many flagpoles around the north entrance to the tunnel and pictures of the Royal couple and the Queen herself were in abundance along the Royal route. The colourful bunting everywhere added to the celebratory atmosphere. The people of Poplar, most wearing their Sunday best clothes were out in force as they lined the streets around the tunnel to welcome the Royal visitors. The Royal couple may have been the main attraction, but the locals were also treated to the sight of many dignitaries as they paraded around in their fancy dress coats and top hats. Will of course, along with the rest of the Bridges Committee were on hand to witness the grand opening. It was a fine day and a great success.

"Well that was a pleasant way to spend a Saturday gentlemen." Will said to his Bridges Committee colleagues as the ceremony came to a close and after the Royal visitors had left. I think William did a great job with the organising, wouldn't you say?"

"He did indeed," agreed one of the committee; a large, heavy built man with a thick moustache and a red face; his voice somewhat higher than his large build suggested. "By the way, Will," he continued, "The amount of work that you've put into the project hasn't gone unnoticed. Have you seen the latest edition of 'The Municipal Journal'? There's a great piece in there about you."

"About me!" exclaimed Will. "I didn't know that."

His colleague smiled, "Well it just so happens that I tore out the page and brought it along today to show you just in case you hadn't seen it."

"Splendid!" cried another committee member. "I haven't read it yet either. Read it aloud will you so we can all hear it."

The first committee member cleared his throat and began to read from the unfolded piece of paper in his hand. "This is taken from the special Blackwall Tunnel edition of the Municipal Journal and the piece is called 'The men who made the tunnel'.

"Mr. Will Crooks, more than any other man, has made Londoners acquainted with the tunnel. His popular lecture on Blackwall Tunnel has

115

been given in all parts of London to all kinds of audiences, and everywhere the clear, picturesque description Mr. Crooks has given, aided by the lantern and his own genial wit, has made intelligible to Londoners, old, young, rich, and poor, what is after all, a somewhat dry and difficult subject.

This only goes to show how closely Mr. Crooks himself has been identified with the construction of the tunnel. As one of the representatives of the Poplar district, he has turned his membership of the Bridges Committee to good account by giving to the tunnel his special attention. No Councilor has been so frequent a visitor to the various works, and it is doubtful whether any outsider went so many times into the compressed air.

The workmen had just cause to bless the Poplar County Councilor. It was owing to Mr. Crooks' efforts that a revised schedule of wages was adopted. The result of this was that the contractors paid an additional £26,000 in wages. With all his zeal for the workmen, Mr. Crooks never once came in conflict with either the contractors or the engineers. Men and masters at Blackwall have all held the worthy Labour Councilor in the highest regard, and both are sorry that their long and cheerful connection must now be severed."

"Well done old chap," came the chorus of approval from his committee colleagues as they slapped him on his back in congratulatory style. Will, however, only felt embarrassed by the attention. "Really gentlemen, I'm only doing my job," he told them.

Back at Spring Gardens at the next meeting of the committee, William Bull, the Chairman announced that he was leaving the Bridges Committee. Will, because of his impressive work during the Blackwall Tunnel project was then elected to take over as the new Chairman.

In his first meeting as Chairman, Will addressed his fellow Bridges Committee members.

"Gentlemen, I'd like to thank you all for electing me Chairman. As Chairman I am excited that there are two projects that I plan to push through this council and through the House of Commons and both are for more tunnels under the Thames. One will be a tunnel for foot traffic only, and this will run between Greenwich and the Isle of Dogs at Island Gardens," (as chairman of the LCC Parks Committee, Will had been responsible for buying an unused piece of land next to the Thames and creating the Island Gardens; a 'little paradise' for local people as he had called it. Will himself formally opened the gardens on August 3rd, 1895. The gardens which included Plane trees, Thorn trees, Holly, Almond, and Flowering Cherry stood in stark contrast to the wharves, factories and run down housing that were its neighbours. It stood out like an oasis in the surrounding greyness). "This tunnel will be known as the Greenwich Foot Tunnel. The other will be for general traffic along the lines of the Blackwall Tunnel between Shadwell and Rotherhithe, and this will be known as the Rotherhithe Tunnel. Once these plans have been passed by Parliament and work on them completed, then we can look into building a similar foot tunnel under the Thames that will connect Woolwich with its neighbours across the river in North Woolwich. I guess this one should be called the Woolwich Foot Tunnel."

32

1898

Will sat in the large high backed chair in the middle of the seated line of Poplar Guardians as they took stock of the woman standing in front of them with her young children. Will's new chair and positioning in the line of Guardians reflected his new status as Chairman. The woman standing in front of them with her young children reminded Will of his own mother all those years before when he had stood by her side clinging fearfully to her skirt. As scared as they had been, his mother had bravely stood in front of those intimidating and grave looking men and refused to listen to their suggestion that her children be put in the workhouse and took them home instead, even though the respite was short lived. Will couldn't help but smile inwardly at how much the system had been improved since he and Lansbury had taken their places on the Board of Guardians. He knew for sure that the woman and her children standing in front of him were scared, but the current Board of Guardians had humanised the system to the point that separating the family and sending them to the workhouse would be their last resort.

As Will walked home on that chilly early evening, he did what he enjoyed best, he stopped and talked to the people that he represented. To the shopkeeper taking in his wares from the front of his shop at the end of his day, Will would discuss the day's business. With the women that stood on their doorsteps chatting, Will would stop and discuss anything from the price of groceries, to problems with their landlords. To the working men that he passed on their way home from work, Will would listen with a friendly ear to their grievances at work and to their problems at home. Will loved the daily interaction with these ordinary people and always seemed to find a word of encouragement for the flagging spirit, or a friendly hand on the shoulder in commiseration for those he couldn't help. His good humoured nature, natural wit and genuine willingness to help, not only put people at ease, but also won their trust and respect.

As Will left the people of Poplar behind that evening and drew closer to his home on Northumberland Street, his thoughts returned to the woman that he had dealt with earlier that day that had reminded him so much of his own mother. That he had been able to help the woman today was primarily down to his own mother he reminded himself. She had been the major influence on his life. She had made sure that he received a proper education, was responsible for his trade, passed on her strong Christian beliefs to him, and even at the age of 76 she still tried to help out when she could with his own children. He smiled happily at the thought of her.

When he entered his house, Elizabeth met him in the hallway. He knew immediately by her expression that something was wrong.

"What is it?" he asked.

"Will," she said, gently. "Your mother's passed away."

33

"Hello love!" Elizabeth called from the kitchen when she heard Will return home from a day at the LCC. "How was your day?" she asked. Will removed his hat and jacket and hung them on hooks on the back of the street door and then went to join her in the kitchen. "It was good," he told her. "I received a letter from Henry Chaplin. You might remember him as being President of the Local Government Board. Well now he's part of Lord Salisbury's Cabinet and he's invited me to be one of the Local Government Board's representatives on the Metropolitan Asylums Board."

"What does that board do?" asked Elizabeth as she filled a heavy looking saucepan with water.

"Here let me finish that for you," he told her as he ignored her question for the moment and took over filling the pan. As he lifted the heavy water filled saucepan onto the stove he replied, "The Asylums Board is quite an important body, although the only time people tend to hear of them is when there is an epidemic of some sort, but it has far reaching powers I've been told. It's the largest hospital authority in the world and includes 14 infectious disease hospitals with accommodation for nearly 7000 people. It maintains 6000 imbecile patients in four asylums and it's also responsible for the welfare of over 2000 children in various homes. It's a select band indeed that's selected to sit on that board and all members need to be nominated by London Boards of Guardians, or by the Local Government Board."

"I'm guessing it's not the type of board that usually sees a Labour man then," said Elizabeth.

"Indeed not," Chuckled Will.

"Do you have time to serve on another board?" she asked. "The LCC and the Poplar Guardians take up so much of your time as it is."

"True!" said Will, "But I see it as a great opportunity to help those poor afflicted people. Plus of course I have the chance to help all those poor neglected children too. Now that is especially appealing."

"So you'll accept then?" asked Elizabeth, smiling, knowing her husband well enough by now to know the answer already.

"Oh yes!" was his reply.

In May, 1898, Will attended his first Asylums Board meeting. The other board members clearly did not know what to make of a working class man in such an exclusive position. "You're that new Labour man aren't you?" asked one of them, barely disguising the contempt in his voice.

"That's correct!" replied Will, politely ignoring the other man's tone.

Where there's a Will, there's a way

"Who nominated you for this board anyway?" the man asked, sounding like there surely must have been a mistake somewhere for a working man like Will to be nominated.

"Henry Chaplin," said Will.

"Henry Chaplin!" the man exclaimed, clearly taken aback by this statement. "But he's a Conservative!"

"That's right!" said Will, taking great joy at the shocked and confused look on the gentleman's face. "Excuse me will you?" he added. "I need to find my seat as it's my first time here." Will walked away smiling as his new board colleague stared after him in stunned silence.

The other members of the board were just as confused by Will's presence. As a Labour member they expected him to be loud in his criticism of the way business was carried out by their select group, but for the first few months, Will did not say a single word at the meetings.

As Will was leaving the building after one of the meetings was over, one of the other board members walked out with him and said in a friendly tone, "You know, Crooks old chap, you're not at all what I expected from a Labour man. To be honest, I expected lots of hostility and criticism from you. I'd even heard you referred to as 'the ranter from the left', but you haven't said a single word yet at the meetings. What's your game old chap?" he asked.

"I'm just learning the business," Will told him with a smile. "This is an old established board with notions of its own and it's not going to be dictated to by a newcomer." But then he grinned widely through his thick black beard and added with a twinkle in his eye. "But just you wait my friend; before long I'll be getting my own way in everything here." And so it was.

34

The Robert Browning Settlement was one of the settlement movements which started in the East End of London at Toynbee Hall in 1884, which were popular in late nineteenth century Britain and the USA. These settlements encouraged university graduates and the middle classes to live and work in deprived areas to alleviate the suffering of the poor. Walworth, in South East London, where the Robert Browning settlement was located, had the highest proportion of paupers in the country.

In 1894, the Reverend Francis Herbert Stead felt compelled to give up his comfortable home in Crouch End, along with his job as a journalist and moved his family across London to Walworth to become warden of the Robert Browning Settlement. As warden, the Reverend was responsible for organising a wide range of recreational and educational activities for the benefit of the community.

In the small, simply furnished room of Browning Hall that he used as his office, the Reverend Stead stood by the open window and with barely contained excitement finished reading the newspaper article in his hands. "Bessie, my dear!" he exclaimed, as his wife and total support system entered the room holding a tray of tea. "Could you try and find me the address of the New Zealand High Commission here in London?"

"The New Zealand High Commission? Why on earth do you need that?" she asked, puzzled.

"I've just read the most amazing article. After all my years of talk about how we need a state run old age pension scheme, New Zealand is to introduce one of their own. I'm going to ask the Agent General if he will come to Browning Hall and explain the system. I plan on inviting trade unionists and others that I know are interested in a national pension system to hear about the New Zealand scheme."

Bessie as ever, calm and refined, made space on her husband's desk and placed his cup of tea there. "That's wonderful news, dear. I'll get on it straight away." The Reverend's mind, however, was already racing with the names of people to invite. He reached for a sheet of writing paper and began penning his letter to the Agent General. When he had finished that task he started writing down his list of people to invite should the Agent General accept his invitation. The first name to make it on to the list was Charles Booth. He decided that he would also invite Booth to speak at the event.

Born in Liverpool in 1840, Charles Booth was a successful businessman that had become concerned with the social conditions of the poor. He was inspired by the philosophy of Auguste Comte, the founder of modern sociology and he also became involved in local politics. In 1875, Booth and his wife settled in London. At the time, the ever increasing scale of poverty in the country's major cities was often being (and as Booth himself thought), sensationally reported in the press. In 1885, H. M. Hyndman who had formed Britain's first socialist political party, the Social Democratic Federation published the results of an inquiry into poverty conducted by the Party, which claimed to show that up to 25 percent of the population of London lived in extreme poverty. Booth was angry at reading such a claim and was certain that Hyndman had grossly overstated the case. Because of his first-hand experience at having dealt with the limitations of the then census collection system (In 1884 he took part in analysing census returns for the Lord Mayor of London's Relief Fund), he decided to investigate pauperism in the East End of London himself by recruiting a team of researchers that included his own cousin, the sociologist, socialist and reformer, Beatrice Potter Webb.

Booth published the results of his investigations in 'Labour and Life of the People' in 1889. Instead of proving Hyndman wrong, he was shocked to find that the situation was even worse than originally suggested by Hyndman. Booth's research suggested that 35 percent rather than 25 percent were living in abject poverty. He then used the results of his research to argue for the introduction of Old Age Pensions. The Reverend Stead was unsure whether Booth would attend the meeting, but he knew it would lend the event a significance beyond the Labour movement if he did, thus attracting outside interest, which would further publicise the drive for a national old age pension scheme.

Other names of people that Stead added to his list were:

Will Crooks, Chairman of the Poplar Board of Guardians. Will had often stated the need for a national old age pension scheme.

George Barnes, Leader of the Amalgamated Society of Engineers.

Margaret Bondfield, representing the shop workers union (later to become the UK's first ever woman cabinet minister).

His finalised list held around 40 names that ranged from leaders of the Labour movement, Trade Unions and Friendly societies.

December 13th, 1898. Browning Hall, Walworth, South East London

The meeting was a great success. William Pember Reeves, the New Zealand Agent General had done an excellent job of explaining the workings of the New Zealand pension scheme and Charles Booth did indeed attend and also spoke at the event, and although his view of pensions differed somewhat from the mainly socialist audience, he was a most welcome contributor to the meeting. Booth's vision of a national old age pension scheme called for it to work alongside a stricter Poor Law, which went against what most of the audience believed. However, they did all share the belief that the aged should benefit from an old age pension of some type.

After the meeting, the Reverend Stead stood conversing with his guests. Guest after guest congratulated him on a job well done. "You know," said one of them, "we should repeat this in other cities."

"I think that is an excellent idea," agreed the Reverend. "Let's go and talk to Pember Reeves and Booth to see if they'll be willing to do just that." They were, and successful meetings followed in Newcastle, Durham, Leeds, Manchester and Birmingham.

After the conclusion of these meetings, Will received in the mail a letter from George Barnes, the leader of the Amalgamated Society of Engineers that was also present at the Browning Hall meeting.

"Mr. Crooks, the meetings across the country that followed Browning Hall have been a great success, however, what we need now is to press on with a national campaign that will keep the pressure on the Government regarding old age pensions. I propose we create a body that will take up the fight on a permanent basis; a National Committee on Old Age Pensions. With your experience with the Poor Law and because of your campaigning already for pensions by way of your Poplar Guardianship and Crooks College, I would like to invite you to serve on the committee." Will did not hesitate in sending his reply. "I would be honoured to serve on such a Committee and hereby accept your invitation."

The first ever meeting of the National Committee on Old Age Pensions was held just a few weeks later. After the introductions were made by the committee's chairman, George Barnes, it came to be Will's turn to address the meeting. He pushed back his chair, stood and said, "I'm grateful to have heard the details of the old age pension schemes set out by Mr. Booth and Mr. Pember Reeves on behalf of Prime Minister Seddon, but I have a different vision of a pension scheme.

For two or three generations, the working classes of this country have been asked to vote for Doodle or Foodle and Old Age Pensions. The elector of today, like his father and grandfather before him is still waiting for the fulfillment of the promise. It seems a vain hope. He too, like those before him may die of old age still waiting, perhaps ending his days in the workhouse. Now I for one have got tired of waiting. I've commenced to pay pensions already." A surprised murmur greeted his statement, but he continued. "I maintain that it is both lawful and right to pay pensions through the Poor Law, and I intend to go on paying them, and to urge others to pay them until Liberal and Conservative politicians cease deluding the people by promises and establish a state pension."

This drew a round of applause. However, one committee member asked, "But isn't that just glorified out-relief?"

"Most pensions are," Will responded, and then added, "At the risk of outraging the feelings of economists, I hold that out-relief to the poor is no more degrading than out-relief to the rich. We hear no talk of endangering the independence of Cabinet Ministers or of Civil Servants when they are paid old age pensions." (Under the Political Offices Pension Act of 1869, pensions were instituted for those who had held political office. To obtain such a pension, the applicant must file a written declaration stating the grounds upon which he claims it and that his income from other sources is not sufficient to maintain his station in life).

Will picked up one of the documents that he had previously set out before him on the table and continued speaking.

"It is argued that the poor have the workhouse provided for theirs, true; but was it not Ruskin who pointed out that, and I quote, 'The poor seem to have a prejudice against the workhouse, which the rich have not; for of course everyone who takes a pension from Government goes into the workhouse on a grand scale: only the workhouses for the rich do not involve the idea of work, and should be called play-houses. But the poor like to die independently it appears. Perhaps if we make the playhouses for them pretty and pleasant enough, or give them their pensions at home, their minds might be reconciled to the conditions'."

He set down the document and began again in his own words, "Some people may look down on these veterans of almost endless toil, but don't forget they have made our country what it is. They have fought in the industrial army for British supremacy in the commercial world and obtained it. The least their country can do is to honour their old age. I want to make life in the workhouse less like life in prison and that all worn out old men and women who have friends to look after them, should be kept as far from the workhouse as possible. To do that means granting a pension. Call it outdoor relief if you like, but at the same time then, call the likes of pensions received by Cabinet Ministers outdoor relief too.

At any rate, relief must be on a more generous scale than it usually is if you are going to keep honourable old people out of the workhouse. Failing that, out-relief has a tendency to perpetuate the sweat shop. Also, take note that 'The Aged Poor Commission' of which the King himself was a member, reporting in 1895, called attention to the ill effects of inadequate outdoor grants and suggested that the amounts be increased. Since I prefer to call out-relief a pension, I want to see it as a real pension and not a dole. Inadequate out-relief gives the sweater that overworks and underpays his opportunity. A sympathetic half-crown a week to a worn out old woman making shirts at ninepence the dozen has the effect of dragging the struggling young widow with a family of children down to accepting the same price. It sometimes takes a whole week to earn one shilling and sixpence, so little wonder that the pinch of hunger sends many a young widow to the devil. We may preach that the wages of sin is death, but life isn't worth living at all to many people. An unknown hell has no more terrors to them than an awful earth.

I want to stop this by making it impossible for the old woman to be the unconscious instrument in encompassing the ruin of the young woman. The old woman cannot live on a half crown dole from the Guardians; so to make a shilling or two more she undercuts the young woman, the sweater then gets them both at reduced wages. Now if the old woman deserves help at all, the help ought to be sufficient to keep her without the necessity of falling into the sweater's net and dragging others with her. The help must be a pension on which she can live. It ought not to be a dole on which she starves.

Nearly all pension schemes like most out-relief systems, fix the allowance at a starvation figure. Sums of four or five shillings won't save old people from hardship. We have in the Poplar workhouse old pensioners who received as much as six shillings a week. They found they couldn't live outside on that, and so had no alternative but the workhouse. An old man would struggle on the outside in his one room, selling and pawning his few things bit by bit to eke out a living until he hadn't a stick left. So, although receiving a pension of six shillings a week, he was forced into the workhouse. Let me tell you about a superannuated trade unionist who came before the board the other day. "We understand you have a pension of six shillings a week," I said. "That's right guvnor," he replied, "but how could you pay three shillings a week out of that for the rent on our one room and then you and the wife live on the rest?"

Take another case; a fine looking old woman enters the relief committee room, scrupulously clean, but poorly clad; a splendid specimen of a self-respecting honourable old English woman."

"Now, my good woman, what can we do for you?" I asked.

"Well sir, we've nothing left in the world, and I've come to see if you can assist us?"

"Where's your husband?"

"He's ill in bed today. He's just turned 73. I'm 75 myself. We've been living on his club money until now. He had six months full pay and six months at half pay. That's as much as the club allows. Now we've got nothing. He worked up to a little more than a year ago. At 73 he can't work any longer."

"The board is very sorry," I said, "but the Poor Law practice is to ask old people like you to come into the workhouse."

"Anything but that, sir," pleads the old woman tearfully. "Both of us over seventy; we should feel it so much now after working all our lives. We can look after ourselves outside if you can give us a little help."

"So here you can see," Will said to the committee, "You have an honest, hardworking old couple still faced with nothing but the workhouse, although they have been thrifty and done everything which the political promoters of old age pensions say ought to be done. We made full enquiries, and for a time at least we would meet their wishes and let them live outside. We gave them six shillings a week, and watched the case carefully. We saw that to eke out existence, one by one their articles of furniture were going. Struggle and strive as they did on their six shillings a week, they would have been compelled to come into the workhouse ultimately after a few further stages of this system of scientific starvation if we hadn't found outside help for them from another quarter.

And so I say again that the out-relief should be the pension. There are a lot of old people receiving out-relief grants of four or five shillings. What is the result? They toil and struggle and pine outside on an amount which barely keeps body and soul together. They reach the workhouse at last and as a rule, through the infirmary. That means they break down and have to get medical orders for admission. It has been proved that 30 percent of the people in Poor Law infirmaries are suffering ailments of some kind or other due to want of proper nourishment. This is what I mean when I say that the present Poor Law as Bumbledom would administer it has nothing better to prescribe than scientific starvation to old people who refuse the workhouse. If one is foolish enough to grow old without being artful enough to get rich, this world is the wrong place to be in.

When old age comes to working people, both thrifty and unthrifty have in most instances to turn to one of two things – precarious charity or the Poor Law. Charity is a splendid exercise for many people, but no law or custom exists compelling its practice. Now the Poor Law can be enforced; only it has been used to terrorise the poor. The State sets up a system to save old people from starvation, and then allows it to be used to perpetuate starvation. I say it won't do. So long as we have this system, I'm not going to make the worst use of it, but the best use of it. And I believe in paying old age pensions through the Poor Law. The Poor Law ought not to degrade any more than the Rich Law degrades under which Ministers and officers of the State receive their pensions. Why do I say pay pensions through the Poor Law? Because it is here. It is something to begin with at once. It is the thin end of the wedge of a system of universal old age pensions, free and adequate. I look forward to working as part of this committee and joining you all in the fight for old age pensions for all." And thus begun a decade long campaign for the introduction of national old age pensions.

35

Once Will had become comfortable with the workings of the Metropolitan Asylums Board, he gradually began to insert his will and steer the committee in the direction that he felt was needed. The fact that he was a Labour man was soon forgotten as his fellow board members began to hear the sense in his words and see his genuine concern for his fellow man. They knew that if he believed in something he would fight to see it through by persuasive argument.

After a meeting when the board had again unanimously agreed to back him in his latest proposal, he was followed out by Sir Edwin Galsworthy, the Chairman of the board for many years. "Mr. Crooks, wait up a moment will you," he called.

Will stopped and waited for Sir Edwin to catch up. "What can I do for you, Sir Edwin?" Will asked.

"Just tell me one thing, Mr. Crooks will you? How is it that whatever you ask this board for, you always get?"

Will looked a little surprised by the directness of the question, but then with a playful wink said, "It's because I'm always right, Sir Edwin!"

It was a new century, the 1900's had arrived. When Will attended the Fabian Society's first meeting of the new year, the main topic of discussion was the upcoming conference that was going to be held at the Memorial Hall on Farringdon Street in London. The previous year, a Doncaster member of the Amalgamated Society of Railway Servants, Thomas R. Steels, proposed that the Trade Union Congress being held in Plymouth call a special conference to bring together all socialist organizations and form them into one central body that would sponsor candidates for independent Labour representation in Parliament. The motion was passed by the Congress. It was agreed that the Fabians would send their secretary, Edward Pease to the conference as their delegate representing the 861 Fabian members.

The conference was held on February 26th and 27th at the Memorial Hall. Along with Pease, other notable groups and individual attendees were the Independent Labour Party (ILP), whose leader was Keir Hardie; the Social Democratic Federation (SDF), an organisation led by H.M. Hyndman, and representatives from the Trades Union Congress, including union leaders such as Will Thorne of the transport workers and Ben Tillett, leader of the great dock strike.

After the debate, the delegates passed Keir Hardie's motion to establish "a distinct Labour group in Parliament, who shall have their own whips, and agree upon their policy, which must embrace a readiness to cooperate with any party which for the time being may be engaged in promoting legislation in the direct interests of Labour." This created an association called the 'Labour Representation Committee' (LRC), which was to coordinate attempts to support MPs sponsored by trade unions who would represent the working-class population. Ramsay Macdonald was elected secretary and took on the task of trying to steer all of the different factions of the new organisation in the same direction. The foundations had been set for a 'Labour Party'.

Later that year in October, a general election was held, an election known as the 'Khaki Election' because the main theme of the election was centered on the second Boer War. The election came too soon for the newly formed LRC to campaign effectively, and only 15 candidates were sponsored, but two were successful; Keir Hardie in Merthyr Tydfil and Richard Bell in Derby. Another notable newcomer to Parliament that year elected as a Conservative was a young 25 year old man that had already earned a reputation for his vigorous campaigning and oratory skills; his name was Winston Churchill.

1901

The London Government Act of 1899 was an act of Parliament that reformed the administration of the Capital. The Act divided London into 28 metropolitan boroughs. Bow, Bromley and Poplar now became the Metropolitan Borough of Poplar and in 1900, Will had been elected as a Poplar Borough Councilor.

He hadn't been on the council for long when his new colleagues began to urge him to stand for Mayor. At first, Will would not hear of it. There were only six Labour representatives on the council and even if he received the support of the progressives on the council, it still seemed very unlikely that he would be able to gain enough votes to make him Mayor. To Will, it seemed like a waste of time to put himself forward with little chance of winning when he had other more immediate council issues to deal with. Time and time again he refused their pleadings to stand as Mayor, citing those very reasons, but still his colleagues implored him. At last he could bear it no longer so he agreed to stand, "But on one condition only," he told them.

"What is the condition?" they asked.

"Should I be elected, there's to be no talk of paying me a salary for doing it." The leader of the delegation was quite taken aback. "But Will!" he exclaimed. "Most London borough councils can pay a salary of between £300 to £500 per year to the Mayor." Will nodded in acknowledgement. "I quite understand that, but I feel I can better retain the confidence of the people and better meet the criticisms of opponents by refusing a mayoral grant. A Labour Mayor will be under the microscope from both sides. I want it to be known I'm Mayor for the good of the borough and the people in it and not for the money the post pays."

In January, 1901, her majesty Queen Victoria had died after being on the throne for 63 years and her son, Edward VII was now King. To be Mayor in coronation year seemed to be the goal of half the councilors in the country. The contest to be Mayor of Poplar was no exception. On election night in November, 1901, the council chambers were unusually crowded as councilors and the supporters of the Mayoral candidates packed the chamber and public galleries to hear the result.

After the initial round of voting was complete, the candidates were whittled down to two. To Will's surprise he was one of the two. The voting for these final two candidates was a tense affair in the noise filled chamber as supporters of both men argued amongst each other in favour of their candidate. If the result of the ballot had been in the hands of the public crammed into the building then Will would have won hands down as his supporters continued to arrive and lend their support as the result was awaited.

When the votes were all in, they were passed to the retiring Mayor to announce the result. He stood and called for silence in the chamber and at last everyone settled down. "We have a tie!" he announced. There was uproar in the chamber. "Gentlemen, gentleman, please I implore you to settle down. The vote will have to be recast. I do not want to use my vote to decide the winner so I implore the chamber to elect a clear winner this time."

As the crowd went back to arguing on behalf on their candidates, the votes were recast and then recounted. At last the outgoing Mayor appealed for quiet. "Gentlemen!" he announced. "We still have a tie." Again there was uproar. When the chamber had settled down yet again, the Mayor announced. "I really do not want to be the one that chooses the new Mayor as I will not be here after my term has finished, so it seems unfair that I cast the deciding vote. We shall have one more vote and I implore you again gentlemen to choose an outright winner."

Again the votes were recast and recounted and yet again the Mayor called for calm. By now the number of people waiting for the result had filled not only the council chamber and the public gallery, but the whole downstairs of the building was now packed solid and people were now spilling out onto the street.

As more workers passed by on their way home from work and witnessed the commotion, they too added their numbers to the swelling crowd and waited for the result to be announced. Up until now the crowd had been noisy with excitement as they waited for the result, but now the tension was getting to everyone and an eerie silence befell both those waiting inside the building and those gathered outside beneath the street lamps.

Back inside the chamber it was no surprise when the result was announced. "Another tie," was the news, but this time the news spread through the crowd in no more than a whisper because of the tension. The retiring Mayor sighed heavily and it was clearly audible in the quiet chamber. "I still do not think it is fair that I should determine the next Mayor." He held up two pieces of paper.

"What I am going to do is write down the name of a candidate on each of these pieces of paper and the name that I draw out will be the new Mayor."

Outside, news of this filtered through to the assembled crowd. The silence was then overwhelming as the men stood waiting for the result; some stood silently praying while others nervously wrung their hands and flat caps.

The silence was suddenly shattered by a huge roar from inside. The doors to the public chamber flew open and men were screaming, "Crooks has got it! Our Will is Mayor!" The crowd outside erupted as they heard the news. The men congratulated each other and cheered as loud as they could. Even some of the burliest workers gathered there were not ashamed of the tears they cried that night. Something momentous had just happened, a working man, one of their own, had just become the first ever Labour Mayor in London.

"God bless the Mayor!" the crowd began to chant. "God bless the Mayor!"

The next day, Will was out walking the streets of Poplar as he always enjoyed doing, stopping here and there to chat with the people that he represented, listening to their stories and complaints. "I say, Mr. Crooks," called a frail looking woman that was standing outside a tenement building as he passed by, "Congratulations on becoming Mayor."

"Why thank you. And how are you today?" Will asked.

"If you can spare a few minutes I can show you," she said.

"Of course I can, madam. What's the problem?"

She led him into her home and showed him the hole in the floor. "Why don't you ask the landlord to repair it?" Will asked.

"I did tell him about it," she sighed, "but he only said, 'What!' the floor fallen in? Why you must have been walking on it!"

Will shook his head, but he felt like shaking his fist. It upset him greatly to see that people had to live in such conditions. "I can assure you that I am going to do all in my power to stop such things happening and bring greater accountability for landlords. We must have laws and standards in place to stop this kind of thing."

As Will continued his walk he stopped off at the market in the High Street and perused the stalls acknowledging the calls of well-wishers when people recognised him. One stall caught his attention and as he stood there looking at its wares, he heard a woman stall holder behind him talking to the neighbouring stall holder. "What d'you think then? They've made that common fellow Crooks, Mayor. And he no better than a working man."

"Quite right, madam," Will said, turning and raising his hat to her. "I am indeed no better than a working man."

Although most of the working class of London were elated at the election of Will as Mayor, the other Mayors of the Capital thought him beneath them. They saw him as a common working man who had no place rubbing shoulders with gentleman Mayors.

Shortly after being elected, Will received an invitation from the Lord Mayor of London, Sir Joseph Cockfield Dimsdale, to attend a conference at the Mansion House; the Lord Mayor's grand, official residence in the City of London. Along with the other metropolitan Mayors, Will was being invited to discuss arrangements for King Edward VII's Coronation dinner for the poor, due to take place in July, 1902.

When Will arrived at the Mansion House, it was clear that the other Mayors intended to give him the cold shoulder for being a Labour man. When the discussions started, Will patiently sat for an hour listening to all sorts of suggestions put forward by men that quite obviously had no understanding of the lives of the poor or what they needed. When at last a break came in the suggestions he stood to offer the Mayoral gathering his own input, but before he could utter a word, a howl of disapproval filled the room. "Sit down!" the other Mayors cried. "Who are you? We want none of your opinions here. Sit down now!" Every time Will tried to speak the howls of disapproval drowned him out. When the howling Mayors realised that the Lord Mayor himself was now on his feet they calmed down and heard him pleading with them to be quiet.

"Gentlemen!" he cried, clearly annoyed. "I protest against this conduct directed at Mr. Crooks."

One of the Mayors was clearly in a state of over excitement and in utter disgust said, "Really Lord Mayor, 'I' protest! What is a Labour man doing discussing the Kings business?" The Lord Mayor was stern in his reply. "I'll have you know, sir, that Mr. Crooks is a personal friend of mine and that we have been colleagues on the county council for the last three years and he, sir, has as much right to be here as yourself as you are both elected officials. Now please, no more of this nonsense and let Mr. Crooks speak."

Knowing that Will and Sir Joseph were actually friends and having been put firmly in his place, the disgruntled Mayor sat down. Will was then allowed to voice his own suggestions regarding the King's Dinner for the poor.

38

As Mayor, Will kept his promise to the woman with the hole in her floor and began his clampdown on landlords. He was going to do all in his power to improve the living conditions of the poor. So many of them lived in squalor and whole families were often reduced to living in a single room, such as he himself had done when he was a child. As Mayor, he intended to take tougher action against the slum landlords. He pushed for pressure to be put on landlords to make repairs to their properties, which up until then they had been able to ignore. This included replacing faulty, foul smelling drains, which would often affect the health of those living near them. He understood that the cost to the council of preventing the existence of slums was small compared with the later cost to the Poor Law authority when it had to pick up the pieces of the broken down people that the slums created.

It had been far too easy for landlords to ignore such upkeep in the past, as many rented out their properties via agents and it was a rare event indeed when a landlord would pay for any repairs in a slum property, which is why up until then, the landlord business had been such a profitable one. In fact, most landlords had never even set eyes on their rental properties. Will did all he could to make the landlords bring their properties up to a decent standard. There was of course a lot of resistance from the landlords so used to being left alone to collect their easy pickings, but Will had the Law on his side and he used it to its full effect to bring the landlords into line.

Even as Mayor, Will carried on his College at the dock gates. He was there one Sunday morning when he addressed the gathered crowd regarding his drive to improve the housing in the Borough.

"Why is it slum property has paid so well in the past for its landlords? It's because it has been neglected that's why. Nothing has been spent on ordinary repairs. Whatever expense we as a Municipal Council may put the owners to in order to make their property healthy is strictly regulated by law. The reason why investors in slum property have reaped such a rich harvest in the past is because neither they nor the local authorities have carried out the law.

No man with ordinary sentiment can own slum property and collect his own rents. A flint hearted agent generally has control. I know such a one well. If the tenant does not pay up by Saturday, he waits and watches round the corner on Sunday morning. As soon as he sees the wife turn out to buy a piece of meat or a few vegetables from a coster's stall for Sunday's dinner, he pounces down on her and demands her few pence on account. It's so easy to run away from responsibility by simply saying, 'This is a mere investment, and I am not concerned with the tenants.'

A very wealthy man who owns a lot of small houses in Poplar had his attention called to the hardship inflicted by the heavy increase in rents. He was told that a widow whose rent had just been doubled would have to seek parish relief if the new demands were enforced. 'My dear good fellow,' said the owner, 'I leave these matters to my agent. I don't want the woman's money. Look here,' pulling a handful of sovereigns out of his pocket. 'Why should I care about the woman's rent? I leave these trifles to my agent and never interfere.'

Can you wonder that so many of our people are driven to drink and immorality? Sweated as they are for rent in this way, they begin to live in an unholy state of overcrowding. House speculators gamble with the people's homes. Nearly every time a house changes hands the rent is raised. The overcrowding is thus made worse than ever. The family living in three rooms takes two. The family in two rooms pushes its furniture closer together and goes into one. Surely something should be done by the State to prevent this gambling with poor people's rents. I would like to see Fair Rent Courts, where the rents could be fixed in fair proportion to the value of the house. Something of the kind has been done in Ireland; why not in England?

One thing is certain; the more crowded the home is, the more convenient becomes the public-house, with its welcome light and deceptive cheerfulness tempting the wretched. Of course, in theory it is easy to argue that the poorer the man the more reason there is that he should not place in the publican's till the money that ought to be spent on food. I fear few of us would retain the moral courage to resist if we had to eat, live, and sleep in the same room, sometimes even in the company of a corpse for several days."

Shortly after the conference at the Mansion House, the Lord Mayor invited Will to join a small sub-committee to oversee the final arrangements for the King's dinner for the poor. The Lord Mayor told Will that Sir Thomas Lipton who had been representing the King at the Mansion House meeting had said that Will was the only Mayor in London who seemed to know what was wanted by the poor. The Lord Mayor also informed him that the King was making £30,000 available to feed the 500,000 poor guests.

As well as having a great deal to do with the organising of the King's dinner for the whole of London, Will did not neglect the local arrangements for the poor of Poplar. 25,000 of the borough's poor were invited to dine. 3000 of these were to be fed under a great awning in the Tunnel Gardens. Planks of wood were ordered and made into long benches and tables; the tables then covered in white tablecloths. Entertainment had also been arranged for the diners in the form of variety artists, pianists, singers and music hall performers. The excitement the dinners were generating in the East End was already high, so when the King announced that he wished to visit Poplar during their dinner, people could talk of little else.

However, shortly before the dinners were to take place, news came that the King had been taken ill with appendicitis. When it was clear that he was too ill to leave Buckingham Palace to visit the diners, the Prince of Wales (later to be King George V) and Mary, Princess of Wales stepped in to take his place.

Saturday, July 5th, 1902

The weather on the day of the dinner was beautiful and 3000 of the borough's poor filed into Tunnel Gardens and took their seats. Then came the food; mutton, veal, boiled beef, ham, meat pies, cheese, bread, potatoes, chocolate and plum pudding were all served, along with beer, ginger beer and lime juice to wash it all down. Along with the free meal, the King had also asked that a souvenir be given to each of the diners as a memento of the day.

Will, dressed in his Mayor's gold laced hat and scarlet robe accompanied by Elizabeth moved among the crowd of diners welcoming them and stopping to chat whenever he could. Many couldn't help but tease him in his fancy get up.

Under the great awning, large banners were hung, which read 'God save the King', and Union Jacks of all sizes were also hung adding colour to the festivities. The sound of laugher filled the air as the poor helped themselves to the treats laid out before them. It would be a long time before they would ever, if ever, sit down to a feast like this again. As the meal came to an end and the diners were getting ready to enjoy the entertainment; a great commotion took place as the Prince and Princess of Wales's carriage arrived, accompanied by a large escort of Horse Guards.

Will and Elizabeth, as the Mayor and Mayoress, welcomed the Royal couple. Will had received a lot of teasing from his fellow Poplar folk when they saw him in his fancy hat and robe, but they were filled with pride when they watched him at ease greeting the Royal guests on the their behalf.

"I bring good news!" The Prince of Wales told the diners. "The operation was a success. The King is out of danger and will recover." It was a perfect message for a perfect day. The diners cheered and raised their souvenir cups to toast the King. "God save the King!" they cried.

40

The children were now getting older and life at 28 Northumberland Street was getting a little cramped for the family, especially as Will was now getting constant visits from local people asking him for help regarding all types of matters that ranged from council issues, Labour questions, job advice and even personal and marriage advice. For these reasons, Will and Elizabeth decided to search for somewhere else to live.

They found a house close by in Gough Street that seemed promising, which had one more room than the house in Northumberland Street, but word around the borough had spread that Will was on the move and one day while still at Northumberland Street, Will received a visitor. The man was an admirer of the work that Will was doing in Poplar and had come to offer Will a house, rent free in East India Dock Road. The large house also boasted a nice front and back garden.

"Please Will, I implore you to accept this offer. I give it to you rent free for the rest of your life. Just look at it as a small tribute from one who appreciates the splendid public services you have rendered to Poplar."

"I'm very touched by the offer, but I must decline." Will told him. "It would never do for me to live in such a house. On one hand my friends among the working people would fear I was deserting their class and would not come to me as freely as they come now, and on the other hand my enemies would say 'Look at the fellow, Crooks; he's making his pile out of us'. A Labour man like me must leave no openings for his enemies."

81 Gough Street, therefore, with its one extra room then became the new Crooks family home.

41

"If Will Crooks' home had a brass plate on the door it would read 'Inquire within upon everything'," said Mr. George R. Sims of the Daily Chronicle, for it was well known in Poplar that between the hours of 9.30 a.m. and 10.30 a.m. Will was available to receive visitors. These visitors, however, were not social callers, but ordinary people of the borough in need of help or advice in all manner of subjects.

At 9.30 a.m. promptly comes the rap, rap, rap on the heavy door knocker that starts the ball rolling. True to his happy nature, Will always greets his visitors with that friendly smile and cheery disposition. "And what can I do for you today?" asks Will of his visitors.

"Hello, Mr. Crooks," said the middle aged woman that was the first visitor of the day. "Do you think you could have a word with my eldest boy. He holds you in such good standing that I think he might listen to you. There's an opening at his dad's work place and we want to get him in there while there's an opening, but he doesn't want to know about work. He thinks me and the old man are going to keep him forever that one, but we're not. He's at that stage where he won't listen to us."

Will smiled sympathetically and put a friendly hand on the woman's shoulder to reassure her and said, "You know, the world can be divided into two classes: some willing to work and the rest willing to let them. Why not tell your boy I'd like a word and if he comes around I'll talk it over with him."

The next visitor, an elderly lady tells Will she's about to be evicted from her home so he gives her the name of a person at the council that may be able to help her and as soon as she leaves another visitor is waiting to be seen. The middle aged man asks Will how he can get his ailing mother into a convalescent home.

The next visitor; an embarrassed looking man tells Will that his wife has kicked him out of the house after coming home drunk again and could Will pay her a visit and try to sort things out with her so he can go home. Of course he will, but not before Will has him promise to scale back on his drinking. And so it goes on, thus the people of Poplar not only have a leader among them, but also a friend.

42

There was a light knock on the street door one evening and Will said, "I'll get it," as he got up from his armchair. He opened the door and then looked down at the small dark haired girl standing on his doorstep in the day's fading light. She wore a dark brown homemade knitted cardigan, which covered a faded dress that was a much lighter shade of brown. She seemed to be around 9 or 10 years old, so Will looked around to see if she was with anybody else, but she appeared to be alone. He looked back down at her and she looked up at him with big hazel eyes and asked shyly "Are you Mr. Crooks?"

"Why yes I am, little lady. What can I do for you?"

"If you please, sir, Fathers took to drink again and Mother says will you come around and give him a good hiding?"

43

Christmas, 1902

On Christmas eve, as Will walked home along Commercial Road in the early evening darkness, he smiled as he passed the shops that were decorated and ready for Christmas. Although it was barely 6 p.m. the darkness had already settled in for the long cold night ahead. A light fluttering of snow began to fall to add to the festive air. Most of the shops were still open to allow for any last minute Christmas shoppers, and lights shone brightly from their windows.

"Hello Will!" called the butcher as he was taking down a goose that was hanging just inside the doorway of his shop. A mother and her children stood further back inside the shop watching the butcher intently as he took down the bird that was to be their Christmas dinner. For most of the poorer people in the area, Rabbit would suffice as the main Christmas dinner and the butcher still had a few of them hanging in his window. Will waved at the butcher and called, "Merry Christmas!"

Just ahead of him, illuminated by the light of the lamp post that they were crowded around, a small group of children stood singing carols. Most of them looked freezing as they rubbed their hands together; their noses red from the cold. None were dressed properly for the cold, but Will knew that these were poor children and that they would be grateful for any clothing, no matter how scant.

Will threw some pennies into the cap that lay on the ground in front of them and stood and listened as they sang "We wish you a merry Christmas and a Happy New Year." As he listened, the wonderful and unmistakable smell of roasting chestnuts reached him and he breathed in deeply to savour the aroma. He noticed that just ahead a vender was roasting and selling them. When the carol was over he walked across to the chestnut vender.

"What can I get for you, Mr. Crooks?" asked the vender.
Will looked back at the carollers. "Hmm, I think five cones should do it please," he said.

"Five coming right up," the vender said.
As the vender took a piece of newspaper and rolled it up into a cone and filled it with hot chestnuts, Will called across to the carollers to come over.

"Here you go, these'll warm you up a bit," he told them. "Just make sure you all get an equal share."

"Thanks guvnor!" they cried, not quite believing their luck. When the vendor had passed on all five cones filled with chestnuts, Will paid him and then wished them all a merry Christmas.

"Merry Christmas to you too guvnor!" the children cried as they tucked into their hot chestnuts.

When Will reached Gough Street he was surprised to see a horse and cart parked outside his home. There was a large wooden crate on the cart and the driver and his young companion were obviously having a hard time lifting it off.

"It's a bit late for deliveries isn't it gentlemen?" Will asked.

"Actually guv, we've been here a little while now. We're having a bit of trouble getting this off the cart. It weighs 300 pounds and we had help loading it on, but now there's only me and the young lad here we can't get the blasted thing off."

"Where's it going?" asked Will.

"Just over there to number 81, to a Mr. Will Crooks."

"Really?" asked Will. "That's me. What's in the crate?"

"Couldn't tell you guv. We just deliver."

"Let's see if we can get it off with my help then," said Will.

Even with three of them it was still a difficult job to get the crate off the cart and then just as difficult a job to maneuver the crate through the doorway into the house where once inside it blocked the hallway.

Now that it was safely inside, the delivery man and boy had done their job and left as quickly as they could to get back home to their families on Christmas eve. Will, surrounded by the whole family managed to pry open the crate and they all stared in amazement at the contents, which was hundreds of plum puddings that had all been squashed together to create a huge mass of pudding. Puddings of various sizes, colours and ingredients had all been used to create the giant mutant one sitting in front of them.

"There's a letter stuck to the inside of the crate!" cried Will's young son, George as he grabbed the letter and gave it to Will.

Still dumbfounded, Will took the letter and began to read it as the family looked on in bewilderment waiting to hear where it had come from.

"It's from the Editor of a newspaper," Will told them. "The newspaper was running a competition for the best plum pudding and were bombarded with puddings and they didn't know what to do with them, so knowing my work with the poor they sent them to me to distribute."

"That's a big pudding," said his youngest daughter, Tilly.

"That's an ugly pudding," said Emily, one of his other daughters as she looked at the huge blob in front of her.

Will looked across at Elizabeth, he was actually speechless for once, but she wasn't.

"Children, quickly mind, get your coats on and get the word out to the neighbours and the surrounding streets that there is free plum pudding to anybody that wants it. Just tell them to bring bowls or pans or whatever they have that can hold pudding."

It wasn't long before the trickle of people arriving turned into a small crowd of people seeking a share of the Crooks' Christmas cheer, however, because of the sheer size of the huge pudding, by the time the crowd began to thin, there was still a great deal of pudding left, so Will hastily arranged for it all to be taken to the Poor Children's Society at Shaftesbury Hall across the river in Borough, South East London, which provided food for the area's poor children. The children at the Hall couldn't believe their luck as they filled their underfed bellies with such an unexpected and tasty Christmas treat.

Part 3

"I believe that generation's yet unborn will in the years to come rise up and call you blessed."

Arnold Hills (Owner of the Thames Ironworks)

44

Early in 1903, Will opened his mail at home as Elizabeth sat across from him reading the morning's newspaper. She liked to keep up with the news, especially the local news that her husband was such an important part of.

"My word!" exclaimed Will as he read the letter in his hand.

"What is it?" Elizabeth asked.

"It's a letter from the Labour Representation over in Woolwich. They want me to stand for Parliament as the member for Woolwich."

"That's wonderful!" Elizabeth cried, "but why Woolwich?"

"I assume it's because of my work on the Bridges Committee and my plans for the Woolwich Foot tunnel. Plus I serve on the Woolwich Ferry sub-committee. So I do have dealings and contacts over the river, but this certainly comes as a surprise."

"Will you stand?" Elizabeth asked excitedly. "Imagine it, Will Crooks MP."

"Now, now, love, don't go getting excited. If I remember correctly, Lord Beresford was returned unopposed at the last election and I believe his predecessor was too. It's a conservative stronghold so the chances of a Labour man winning would be remote."

"When's the next election due?" she asked.

"1906," said Will thoughtfully. "If I accepted, it would give us a few years to prepare and work on a decent campaign."

"So will you do it?" she asked.

Will smiled and said, "You know, I think I will."

Just a couple of weeks later on February 18th, a small deposition from the Woolwich Labour Representation called on Will at home in Gough Street. He welcomed them into his home, but the sheepish manner in which they entered alerted Will to something being amiss. "Whatever is wrong gentlemen? Had second thoughts about wanting me to stand in Woolwich have you?" he asked, only half jokingly. The leader of the trio of Labour men cleared his throat.

"Will, about the three years that we thought we had to prepare for the election. Well... think three weeks instead," he said as he grimaced, expecting Will to explode.

"What do you mean?" asked Will, clearly confused.

"Lord Beresford has been offered the command of the Channel Squadron. The Admiral is resigning from his Parliamentary seat in Woolwich. The by-election is going to be held on the 11th of March. That gives us exactly three weeks to prepare." All three of the Labour men looked anxiously at Will as they waited for his reaction. It surprised them when it came in the form of raucous laughter. "I guess we best start planning then gentlemen." When he had stopped laughing, he asked, "Do we have a plan?"

There was no doubt that the Woolwich Labour Representation had been taken off guard, but they rallied well and quickly managed to raise £200 from its members for election expenses, but it was soon clear, however, that to get their message out to the 16,000 Woolwich voters they would need a great deal more than that. An appeal went out from the Labour Association for donations to help them with their expenses. The Daily Mail newspaper took up the cause, which opened a Woolwich election fund and donations started to pour in from all sections of society. Will threw himself head strong into the fight with his usual good humour and down to earth manner. His magnetic personality soon drew together all factions of the Progressive and Labour movements in Woolwich. The Temperance society and churches of most denominations also backed him in his cause.

His friend and colleague from the dock strike and the LCC, John Burns, already an MP himself, but now aligned to the Liberal Party, went down to Woolwich to speak with Will at a public meeting in the Drill Hall. Over 5000 of the electorate turned up to see them. The huge crowd was far too big for the building, forcing many of them to remain outside in the street blocking traffic and preventing the trams from passing. Inside, Burns told the gathering:

"Woolwich has in Mr. Crooks, a man who not only carries a banner which typifies a cause, but honours the army for which he works. By his tolerance and sweet tempered geniality, he has united progressive forces of Woolwich as they have never been united before. In securing what is possible today, Mr. Crooks never forgets his ideal, but with a brotherly love and Christian charity pursues the line of least resistance in a way which Labour has not always shown."

After Burns had finished speaking, Will thanked him and then took his turn to address the gathering. "Ladies and Gentlemen, I see things are just the same on this side of the river as they are over the other side in Poplar. I've been hearing the same old thing during this short campaign as I did when I ran for Mayor in Poplar. Lovely ladies are still going about with their lovely stories. As they canvass for my opponent they tell the elector or his wife that the rates will go up if a Labour candidate is elected. They say that because he is a poor man he will have to be paid a salary of £500 a year out of the rates. Well let me tell these alluring ladies that Will Crooks has been in public life for 14 years and has never had a penny from the rates in all that time. I tell them further that if I remain in public life for another 50 years, I still will never take a penny from the rates.

I was asked a very good question the other day in Woolwich. A kindly old lady asked me why I wanted to enter Parliament. Well I have no desire to enter Parliament unless it be for the opportunities it may afford me of continuing and extending my life's work. If I can further the well-being of my country by assisting in the developing of a nation of self-respecting men and women, whose children shall be educated and physically and mentally fitted to face their responsibilities and duties, I shall be content.

I therefore ask those of you that believe that the greatness of our empire rests on the happiness and prosperity of its people to consider carefully the importance of the present election. I am of the opinion that a strong Labour Party in the House of Commons, comprised of men who know the sufferings and share the aspirations of all grades of workmen is certain to exercise greater influence for good than the academic student.

Mr. Drage, my opponent tries to justify low wages paid to many in the Woolwich Arsenal by saying that 'half a loaf is better than no bread.' Well let me tell you good people, they'll be no half-loaf policy for us: we want the whole loaf." The audience loved what they heard and cheered him enthusiastically.

The Daily Mail's Woolwich fund raised £1000, which went a long way to help get Will's and the Labour Association's message out to the voters of Woolwich.

Polling day (March 11th) quickly arrived and the loaf of bread became a focal point of the election. Will's supporters took to the streets with full loaves of bread stuck on top of poles showing their support for the Labour policy. The bakers of Woolwich had made thousands of miniature loaves about the size of a walnut with stalks through them so that they could be attached to clothing. They were being sold in the street and in shops for a penny each and everywhere you looked people seemed to be wearing one. Men wore them in their button holes, boys wore them in their caps and women pinned them to their dresses. There was quite a party atmosphere building and Will's supporters actually began to feel like a victory was possible, however, it was not forgotten that before the last uncontested elections in Woolwich, the Conservatives had won the seat with majorities of over 2000 votes at both of the previous two elections when they had faced an opponent.

As the day of voting drew to an end, Will, Elizabeth and the leaders of the Labour Association made their way to the town hall to wait for the results. At last, Will and Mr. Geoffrey Drage were called to the podium where they exchanged warm handshakes and then nervously waited for the

Where there's a Will, there's a way

results to be announced. The atmosphere inside and outside the Town Hall was electric. Inside, the noise was deafening. Outside, not only were the street lamps lighting up the night sky, but many improvised torches were lit too, blanketing the many faces of the excited crowd in a flickering glow, which only added to the tense atmosphere.

Back inside, the returning officer after repeatedly calling for silence finally managed to calm everybody down.

"Ladies and Gentlemen!" he announced. "I have the results for the by-election of the constituency of Woolwich. The results are as follows:

Mr. Geoffrey Drage, Conservative, 5458 votes.
Mr. Will Crooks, Labour, 8687 votes."

The crowd erupted inside the hall and the returning officer's voice was drowned out as he announced "By a majority of 3229 votes, Will Crooks is the new Member of Parliament for Woolwich."

As news spread to the crowd outside they too erupted into loud cheers of victory. Will managed to calm things down on the podium as he was congratulated by everyone, including Geoffrey Drage. He then told the crowd, "May I say, now that I am elected the Member for Woolwich, that it will be my aim and desire to serve all sections of the people of Woolwich, including of course, those who voted for Mr. Drage, as well as those who voted for me."

When Will and Elizabeth were finally allowed to leave the Town Hall, it was only with the help of the police who managed to make a passageway between the cheering crowd to the market square where it had been arranged for the winner to address the crowd. When they took to the platform the crowd went wild with excitement. Time and again Will tried to speak, but each time his voice was drowned out by the noise. He tried to call for silence and at last with the help from the Labour organisers among the crowd he managed to succeed. Will seized his moment and said, "Tonight, Woolwich has sent a message of love and hope to Labour all over the country." The crowd erupted yet again, but try as he might, there was no silencing them again. A large bouquet was then passed up onto the platform for Elizabeth. She smiled happily at the flowers and then at Will, the new Member of Parliament for Woolwich. Will took her hand in his and together they stood and enjoyed the cheers of victory.

"The greatest by-election victory of modern times."
William Court Gully – The Speaker of the House of Commons. (Liberal).

45

1903. Crooks College, The Dock Gates.

Shortly after his Woolwich by-election victory, Will addressed his College audience for the first time as a Member of Parliament:

"The workman is learning after years of unfulfilled pledges and broken promises of the usual party stamp that before he can get anything like justice he must transfer his faith from gentlemen candidates to Labour candidates. The workman has seen how the gentlemen of England have treated him in the last few years by taxing his bread, his sugar, his tea; tampered with his children's education, attacked his trade unions, made light of the unemployed problem, and shirked old-age pensions. What the workman has done in Woolwich, you will find he will do in other towns.

Labour representation is quite a natural result of the failure of rich people legislating for the poor. The one hope of the workman is strong Labour representation. The Labour Member has nothing but his service to give in return for support. The continued selection of rich men for working-class constituencies is a perversion of representation, and quite as absurd as it would be to attempt to run a Labour candidate for the aristocratic West-End division of St. George's, Hanover Square."

46

On the north bank of the River Thames, the grand gothic building that is the Palace of Westminster sits at the heart of the great British Empire. Once the residence of the Monarchs of England, it is now home to both Houses of Parliament; the House of Lords and the House of Commons.

Standing at the north end of the building at a height of 350 feet is the majestic clock tower that holds Big Ben, the huge 14 ton great bell of the clock that chimes every hour for the people of London below. Inside the Palace of Westminster itself, in the House of Commons with its rows of traditional green leather seats and surrounded by wood paneled walls sat the men that ran the country and the Empire.

It wouldn't take long before Will's working class roots would be at odds with the university educated majority of those men. Will listened to Mr. Arthur Balfour, the Conservative Prime Minister as he answered another Member's question and then sat back down. Will stood and asked, "Prime Minister, does that mean that the Aliens Bill will take precedence over Redistribution?" Mr. Balfour stood again and replied, "The two things are not at all in pari materia."

Exasperated, Will also stood again. "As the Prime Minister is aware, I have no knowledge of Latin. Will the Right Honourable Gentleman put his answer into English?"

"What I meant to convey was that you could not compare resolutions with a Bill, because a Bill involved a number of different stages, while the other dealt with the matter as one substantive question," the Prime Minister told him.

A voice then called out from the Conservative benches, "A very loose translation if not lucid," which brought laughter to the house.

"Thank you!" Will said, and responding to the laughter he added, "I was busy learning life when you other boys were learning Latin. This learning of life gentlemen, carrying with it an intense love of truth and justice has proved more useful to me and the class I serve than any knowledge of a dead language could."

Outside of the chamber, Will stood talking to a number of fellow MPs when one of them patted him on the back and said, "Good show in there today old boy. I'll mind that I never use Latin in your presence." One of the group laughed and added, "I never enjoyed Latin lessons at university anyway."

"Let me explain something to you gentleman," Will began in a relaxed manner. "My training for becoming a servant of the people has been better than any university training. My university has been the common people. The man trained as I have amid the poor streets and homes of London, who knows where the shoe pinches and where there are no shoes at all, has more practical knowledge of the needs and sufferings of the people than the man who has been to the recognised universities. But do not get me wrong gentlemen, I do not despise education. I have felt the need of more education my whole life, but I do protest against the idea that only those that have been through the universities or public schools are fit to be the nation's rulers and servants.

Legislation by intellectuals is the last thing we want. Look at that recent case under the workman's compensation act where eight leading lawyers argued for hours whether a Well, 30 feet deep was indeed a building 30 feet high. Finally they decided that it was not." In spite of their university educations and the fact that most among them would class themselves as intellectuals, the MPs gathered around him couldn't help but laugh.

47

August 10th, 1904. House of Commons

From his earliest days at his College, Will had argued that all basic education should be paid for out of the Imperial Exchequer, and when he entered Parliament, he argued the case there too. It was quite obvious to him that if you educate all the people of the country, then that will ultimately be for the good of the country. It would give everyone the basic tools to make better their lives and in return improve the standing of the country as a whole. The poor and those living in abject poverty would especially benefit from free schooling. With an education under their belt, the opportunity would be there to lift themselves out of their present condition and make better their lot, while at the same time relieving local authorities of the cost of keeping them when they eventually ended up in the workhouse or on out-relief. However, Will also knew from his own experiences that if a poor child turns up for schooling with hunger pains in his stomach, all the free schooling in the world isn't going to benefit the child if they are so hungry they cannot concentrate on anything but their hunger.

A debate was in progress in the House on recent Minutes issued by the Board of Education that differed in tone from those circulated prior to the Education Act of 1902; a debate which had begun on the Religious aspect of the Act, but which had soon became a wider discussion on the current education system. Two things very close to Will's heart were his love of the Poor, and Children, so when the two subjects came together in the form of Poor Children, Will could not help but become involved. The debate was in full swing when Will rose to add his own voice to the discussion.

"In recent years I do believe that the Education Board has endeavoured to make education a little more attractive, but I will never be content with the educational arrangements of this country until the workman's son and daughter are given the same opportunity as the children of the middle and upper classes. Every child should have the same opportunity of gaining the position he was fitted to fill. A good milliner or dressmaker was almost as valuable to the nation as even a learned professor of Oxford or Cambridge. They are useful to the whole community, and certainly they help to create the wealth of the nation.

Now in regards to dealing with the question of underfed children attending schools. I do strongly urge this House that something should be done in this matter at once, and that it should not be put off until next year. This question has been discussed for years, and it will be postponed yet again and passed on to the Honourable Gentleman from the Education Board's successor if the policy which has been pursued in the past is continued. That would not be a very bright outlook for the poor children. I do not think any special grants should be required to enable them to feed the children who came to school hungry. I believe everlasting credit is due to the people who privately organise schemes for providing free meals, but they are unable to cover the whole ground. We hear the same thing every winter; casual employment, sick father, mother broken down in health and children going to school unfed. In the poorer districts, when the children, who after three years of age have to feed on other food sources instead of maternal sustenance begin to fade away and get weaker and weaker, are they then going to keep these children of from three to five years of age away from school? I sincerely hope not. They will be better cared for in schools than in the slums and courts of the East End. Why should these children be kept on private charity? If anyone went into an infirmary he would be amazed to find the number of young men and women who were absolutely broken down because they were insufficiently fed between five and twelve or fifteen years of age. It would never do to have special classes for underfed children in the schools. That would be to put a badge upon them; and children; be they ever so poor, have some sort of natural pride. Nothing could be easier than to provide two meals a day for all children at the board schools; and it could be done at very little expense. There might be a general rush at first, for the novelty of the thing, but the local authority would very soon be able to gauge to a pound how much the scheme would cost. Some people would, no doubt, say that the parents could feed their children if they were only a little more careful, did not drink so much and spend their wages in riotous living. But, be that as it might, it had nothing to do with the children, and it was the children that they had got to look after. If the Education Department was to have regard to the future, they would have to take up this question of feeding the children as one of the first principles of education.

When it is said that that would relieve the parents of their responsibility, my answer to that is if they did not do this for the children when they were young, they would have to pay for it when they were older and became useless members of society. The House of Commons is the place where some help should be given to these poor little children. They should not be starved for the convenience of the Parliamentary Secretary of the Board of Education, or the Treasury, or the Chancellor of the Exchequer. Their duty is clear that when the children are compelled to go to school, they should be fed to enable them to get some benefit from their education.

I am not alone; there are many people who to their credit insist that it would be a good thing if the feeding of these poor children was part of their school curriculum. If that were done, what a fine race we should grow up, and it would also be found that England did not exist for a few, but for all."

48

Women's suffrage in Britain as a national movement began in 1867 with the formation of the National Society for Women's Suffrage. By the turn of the 20th century, however, little progress had been achieved in this national campaign. In 1903, frustrated by this lack of progress, Emmeline Pankhurst (until recently a fellow Fabian who had resigned from the society in March 1900 because of the society's refusal to oppose the Boer War), and her daughter Christabel, founded the Women's Social and Political Union (WSPU). The WSPU was an all-women suffrage organisation whose motto was 'Deeds, not words'.

August 15th, 1904. House of Commons

Will was very much in favour of votes for women and in August of 1904 he introduced the Women's Enfranchisement Bill, which had been prepared by the Independent Labour Party. He told the House of Commons, "I'm introducing this Bill because in all my public work I aim at making the people self-reliant and able to think and act for themselves. I therefore want women to have the power and the responsibility that the possession of the vote gives. It is by this, rather than by any consideration of how their votes would be used that I ask for woman's suffrage. At the same time I believe that the course of progress has nothing to fear from this reform. We entrust to women as teachers and as mothers the all-important work of educating the future citizens. How absurd, then, to hesitate to give to women the rights of a citizen. As regards the women of the working class, I point out constantly that all the many social questions that are pressing for settlement affect these women as much as, if not more than, they affect their husbands. We must give women a share in settling such questions.

I often tell people the story of an incident when I complained about the low wages paid to women in the Government's food supply yard at Deptford. "It's starvation to pay widows with families 14 shillings a week," I told the official in charge.

"But it's constant!" he exclaimed, clearly surprised that I was complaining about it. So you see gentlemen," Will added, "Government officials think starvation's all right so long as it's constant. Do you think this system of constant starvation would be tolerated for a day if women had the vote?"

Unfortunately, the parliamentary session closed before a second reading was reached, so the Bill died.

The following year, in October, 1905, the WSPU would begin its campaign of disruption in its attempts to win votes for women, prompting the Daily Mail newspaper to derogatorily label the women of this branch of the suffrage movement, 'suffragettes'.

49

The winter of 1904 was fast approaching and the number of unemployed at this time of the year as always was alarming. The East End as usual was being hit hard. As Will left the House of Commons after yet again trying to urge the House that the State should be dealing with the unemployed, a Conservative member walking out with him, said, "This unemployed question is a terrible worry, Crooks."

"Yes," replied Will as the Conservative member stepped into his motor car. "It is a terrible worry when you have it for breakfast, dinner, tea and supper."

As Will made his way back east to Poplar he passed through the thriving West End with its throng of people rushing off to clubland, dinner parties and the theatre. His thoughts turned to the census of the unemployed in Poplar that the Guardians had recently taken, which had found that 24 percent of regular wage earners there were unemployed. "Yes," Will thought to himself. "A terrible worry the unemployed."

In the opening session of Parliament, Will stood and addressed his Right Honourable colleagues as they discussed the unemployed. "Gentlemen," he began jovially, "I know well both the loafer and the man who was born tired. The wife of one such got up early and wakened her husband in time for work.

"Is it raining?" the man asked from the folds of his bedclothes.

'No.'

'Does it look like raining?'

'No.'

'Oh I wish it were Sunday'."

Laughter filled the house, but then with a sudden change in tone, Will became serious. "But what about the upstanding man who through no fault of his own cannot find work when he needs it. I tell you that if an able-bodied man out of a job is driven into the workhouse then he generally remained a workhouse inmate for the rest of his life. It degrades and demoralises him. It takes away his muscle to stand up and fight for himself. If the Local Government Board would permit Guardians to take land, this man could be put to useful work. Even able-bodied men of the 'in-and-out' type would be better put to work on the land under powers of compulsory detention. Of course, these men should be allowed to go out if they really desired to look for other work. What they should not be allowed to do was to drag their wives and children about the country, vagrants bringing up more vagrants.

Employment on farm colonies would quickly get rid of the tramp difficulty. Such men, trained in useful agricultural work, if they felt they had little chance in this country, would then have some equipment for the colonies. A country like Canada for instance, had no use for men who had simply been loafing about English towns, but would very quickly find work for men who had had a little training and discipline on the land. It would be better for the whole community that something of this sort should be done than that we should go on with the present system of doles and relief, whose effects, like idleness, only demoralised."

Will, along with some fellow MPs that were as concerned as he was about the state of the unemployed visited Mr. Long, the President of the Local Government Board.

"As you know, Mr. Long," Will began. "I've been calling for years that the Poor Law unions of London should be allowed to form a central committee so that they can deal with the unemployed as a well organised central body instead of Poor Law unions acting alone, where although their acts to meet unemployment were well meaning, it usually ended in waste and confusion so that the genuine unemployed received little help.

As far back as 1893 I was appealing to the Board of Trade and the Thames Conservancy, asking them to find employment for the unemployed over the long dark workless winter months by reclaiming foreshores. Under the Foreshores Act, the Board of Trade has the power to reclaim land and under a similar Act the Thames Conservancy can reclaim miles of foreshore in and around London. Reclaiming land like this is just the type of work to absorb unskilled labour. This has already been carried out successfully up north where they reclaimed land on the banks of the Forth and Tay and also along the Lincolnshire coast.

Instead of the local Poor Law unions having to raise the rates to pay for out-relief to the unemployed, I strongly believe that these unemployed should be found useful and rewarding work. When I first joined the Board of Guardians in Poplar, the inmates of the workhouse were given the 'task' work of picking oakum and stone-breaking. This was both useless and degrading. In its place we introduced work that was both useful and profitable. Instead of oakum picking and stone breaking, we introduced clothes making, laundry work, baking bread, wood chopping, painting and cleaning. This has the effect of lifting up these workers. It makes them strong as individuals knowing they are doing something worthwhile. Letting these people do meaningless task work and take relief where it's offered is just downright soul destroying. But this was just done in Poplar, paid for by the Poplar rates. I say we need a central committee where all the Poor Law unions can come together and act as one, sharing ideas and sharing the financial burden, although in the long run I intend to continue to lobby Parliament for the Government to take control of the unemployment problem and offer state aid to the unemployed."

At the end of the meeting, Mr. Long said, "Gentlemen, your arguments are compelling. Here is what I propose. I intend to call a conference to discuss the unemployed at the Local Government Board. The earliest that I can arrange such a conference would be in October. Are you satisfied with that in the short term? One of the items on the agenda would of course be to discuss the possibility of creating a central committee."

Mr. Long was good to his word. On October 14th at the Local Government Board building in Whitehall, the conference for the unemployed took place. The Poplar Guardians sent Will and Lansbury as their representatives with a list of carefully prepared proposals.

1. The President of the Local Government Board to combine the London Unions for the purpose of dealing with the unemployed and the unemployable.

2. Such central authority to take over the control of all able-bodied inmates in London workhouses.

3. Farm colonies to be established by the central authority for providing work.

4. Local Distress Committees to be also set up, consisting of members of Borough Councils and Boards of Guardians, to work on the lines already laid down by the Mansion House and the Poplar Distress Committees.

5. The cost to these local committees of dealing with urgent need occasioned by want of work to be a charge on the whole of London or on the National Exchequer, instead of being a charge on the locality, always provided that the payment given be for work done on lines similar to those adopted by the Mansion House and the Poplar Distress Committees.

6. Rural District Councils to be asked to supply the Local Government Board with information when labourers are wanted on the land, such information to be sent to the Local Distress Committees.

7. Parliament to take in hand the question of afforestation, the reclamation of foreshores, and the building of sea walls along the coast where the tide threatens encroachment.

The conference was a success and shortly afterwards, Mr. Long formed a Central Unemployed Committee for London, personally arranging that Will and Lansbury become members. He also introduced local distress committees for the Poor Law and Municipal Authorities.

Although this was good news, the newly formed committees could do little in the time available to provide work during that coming winter. As usual the plight of the unemployed seemed darkest in the East End. For example, West Ham, one of Poplar's close neighbours was in such a state that the Daily Telegraph and the Daily News raised £30,000 in relief. Poplar too was in a similarly bad state of affairs, but the Guardians did all they could to deal with the problem themselves.

One day as the Guardians were taking their seats for a meeting to actually discuss the problem, they became aware of a commotion from outside. The commotion soon exploded into the meeting room as a crowd of angry, starving men burst in. Some of the men were carrying large pieces of wood that were obviously meant to be used as weapons and as a threat to get what they wanted.

"We need help!" they cried angrily. "Our families are starving. For god's sake you have to help us!"

The startled Guardians looked on in shock and fear, but Will got to his feet and calmly approached the men. He stopped in front of them and looked around the room at their poor wretched faces and said solemnly, "Men, I see faces among you that I know well. Some of you I've known for years and it pains me to see all of you in such a desperate state, but please, before you go any further, put down those pieces of wood, you'll not need them here. I've witnessed bread riots before, so believe me, I know how quickly things can get out of hand and innocent people hurt by want of desperation for food."

"But our families are starving, Mr. Crooks!" said one of the men desperately.

"I know they are and that's why we're here now," Will reassured him. "We're here to get relief and food organised for all of you."

"We've been promised help before and look at the state we're still in," said a disgruntled man angrily waving his piece of wood in Will's direction.

"That's right!" was the chorus of approval from the other men around him backing him up.

Will was sympathetic. "Men, the Poor Law is entrusted to myself and these other Guardians here to prevent starvation. A dear friend of mine once said that 'the law that safeguards the poor is always in the hands of those who do not put it into force'. Please believe me when I say that so long as I live that shall not be said of Poplar. I promise you all that your claims will be considered, and urgently too. Please just try to hang on in there. We don't want any of your families forced into the workhouse so we'll do our best to get you the out-relief that you need."

Reluctantly the men retreated and Will was good to his word and out-relief was given, but the rates had to be raised to meet the cost and then there was only enough money for a few shillings worth of food for the men and their families; just enough in fact to keep many out of the workhouse where the cost of their keep to the Borough would have been much, much greater.

In the early hours of the morning, Elizabeth rolled over in bed as she sought a more comfortable sleeping position. Outside, the moon was almost full on a clear, cool night. Its light shone down brightly onto Gough Street below, basking the street and rooftops in an eerie night time brightness.

She wasn't sure why, but when she rolled over she also opened her eyes. The moonlight had found a small gap in the drawn curtains and a slither of light had seeped in through the crack, illuminating the darkened room just enough for Elizabeth to make out Will's outline sitting up in bed. "What are you doing?" she asked.

"Go back to sleep, love, don't mind me. I just can't sleep that's all," he told her, although his voice sounded tired.

"What's wrong?" she asked.

"Nothing's wrong," he assured her. "I've just been trying to think of new ways to help the unemployed, but now my mind is racing when it should be sleeping."

"Do you want me to make you some warm milk to settle you down?" she asked.

"No I'm fine, just go back to sleep," he told her. "I'll lay down again now too. I'm sure I'll fall asleep soon."

But as Elizabeth quickly drifted back to sleep, all Will could do was toss and turn as his thoughts returned to the problem of the unemployed.

Unbeknown to Elizabeth, most of Will's nights had now taken on a similar pattern as he tossed and turned, his mind refusing to relax as he tried to come up with new ways to help those out of work. Will was putting so much effort into the unemployed problem that not only was it taking up most of his time during the day, but it was now taking up most of his nights too. Overwork during the great dock strike had resulted in serious illness for Will. Now once again he was pushing his body to the brink.

When Elizabeth awoke the next morning, Will was still asleep. Although it was unusual for him to sleep in, she decided not to wake him. After being awake during the night, she wanted him to catch up on his sleep. But as the morning wore on and he still hadn't roused she went back into the bedroom to check on him. At first she tried to gently call for him to wake up, but when there was no response she tried calling his name louder. When there was still no response she began to shake him. At last she managed to coax a response, although it was only in the form of a brief moment of consciousness and it was clear that Will was confused and wasn't aware of his surroundings. Elizabeth knew something was seriously wrong, so she called the doctor immediately.

"Just how bad is it doctor?" she asked as he finished examining Will. The doctor removed the stethoscope from around his neck and then placed it in his black medical bag which he then closed with a snap of its clasp. With a glance he indicated that they should talk outside, so Elizabeth led him out of the bedroom and into the hallway.

"I'm afraid he's had a nervous breakdown, Mrs. Crooks," he said gravely. "We need to monitor him to see how severe it is, but I must warn you that if there is no significant change in his condition soon, then we could be looking at confinement to bed for at least 3 months."

When the news spread about Will's condition, an endless stream of well-wishers from all walks of life sent their best wishes and prayers for a speedy recovery.

50

Luckily the change that the doctor was hoping for did come, although the breakdown would have a lasting effect on Will's health.

As the end of January, 1905 approached, Will's health had improved enough for him to travel up to Liverpool to attend the Conference of the Labour Representation Committee. He was particularly looking forward to attending as he had some exciting news to share. He proudly told the Conference that the King's speech at the next opening of Parliament would announce a 'Unemployed Bill'.

And so it was; on April 18th, Mr. Gerald Balfour, who had since replaced Mr. Walter Long as President of the Local Government Board introduced the Bill. The Bill did indeed include the promised scheme of District Committees in London and in other provincial towns. It also agreed the principle of State Aid by allowing the cost of the organisation to be charged to the rates, but leaving it to voluntary subscriptions to provide a fund for paying the men's wages.

After the initial excitement of the Bill passing its second reading with a majority of 217 votes, the Bill then seemed to run out of steam and stalled. There seemed little prospect of it getting through the committee stage and becoming law. Will became increasingly frustrated as the Bill sat untouched and other parliamentary business took precedence over it. When August arrived and the House was just a week from adjournment, Will tried one last push and again brought the matter of the Unemployed Bill up in Parliament, but the Prime Minister, Arthur Balfour, told him and the House that there was no time for the Bill.

Will was not happy. He stood and in reply addressed the Prime Minister and the House. "I admit the Bill's faults and shortcomings as readily as everyone, but it does contain the germ of a great principle – State recognition of the need and State Aid in carrying out the organisation. I urge the House to save the unemployed from foolish and useless rioting by holding out to them the hope which the passing of this Bill would convey. The Prime Minister urges the plea that there is no time. Well what would the businessmen of this House think when they went down to their offices tomorrow, if they were told by the manager that grouse shooting would begin on the 12th and that therefore business would have to be suspended? Does the Government prefer grouse-shooting to finding work for honest men? Was this Bill only introduced to kill time—to wait until the birds were big enough to be shot? I don't want to stop your holidays. Go and kill your grouse and your partridges. But are you going to put dead birds before living men?

On the day when the Eton and Harrow Cricket match is played; what will the unemployed say when they hear that the Government could not find time to discuss this Bill because Ministers wished to see two schools play cricket? Do you think the working man gets a day off to see his sons play cricket in the public parks? Unlike many Honourable Members of this House, workmen do not live by dividends; they have nothing to sell but their labour. When out of work a little help often saves them from ruin and pauperism. They are only asking to be given an opportunity to fulfill the divine curse by earning their living by the sweat of their brow."

As soon as Will sat down, one of his colleagues came across and whispered something to him. Will quickly stood again and announced, "And may I just add gentlemen that I have just been informed that as I speak, the Police in Manchester are charging a desperate crowd of the unemployed."

The Daily News. August 5th, 1905

"The strange story of the passing of the Unemployed Bill.

At the end of last week its chances seemed to have disappeared. Today it has passed committee, and Monday will see it through the Commons. The member chiefly responsible for this issue is Mr. Will Crooks, who has shown undoubted subtleness as a Parliamentary tactician."

Will, along with many others thought the Act came just in time to prevent serious disorder in the larger towns and cities where distress and discontent was running high. The winter that followed the Act was a particularly harsh one for the unemployed. Although the distress Committees that were created under the Act quickly got to work; the London committees found themselves without funds. The weak point of the Act was that it only allowed for the costs of the organising committee to be met by the State. The committees were confused and asked, 'What was the use of organising work for the unemployed when there were no means of paying them wages?' It looked as though the hoped for public subscriptions were not to be forthcoming. It appeared that the hard fought for Act was going to fail at its first hurdle.

This time, however, it was Elizabeth that took up the fight. The wives and women of the Poplar unemployed met in the Town Hall and with Elizabeth in the chair they decided to petition the Government into voting money into the newly founded Distress Committees. It was also decided that the women of Poplar would march to Whitehall to back up their appeal. When news spread of what the women of Poplar were going to do, poor women from places such as Edmonton, Paddington, West Ham, Woolwich, Hackney and Southwark decided to add their support and march side by side with their sisters from Poplar. The women from Southwark were led by Bessie Stead, wife of the Reverend Francis Herbert Stead, whom Will knew from the Robert Browning Settlement and the National Committee on Old Age Pensions.

On November 6th, headed by Elizabeth and the then Mayoress of Poplar, Mrs. Dalton, somewhere close to 6000 women gathered by the Thames on the Embankment near Charing Cross Bridge to begin their march to Whitehall. As the march started the women began to chant 'Work for our men – Bread for our children'. However, it soon became clear that the march was not going to be an easy one; the days leading up to the march had been filled with rain, and although it was now dry, the Embankment had not had time to dry out in the cold November air and was deep in mud. The women, however, having travelled so far to march were not going to be easily deterred, so they trudged on through the mud as best they could. The women that were carrying young children found the going particularly tough as they were unable to lift their skirts to keep them out of the mud and hold onto their children at the same time, so as they struggled on they could only leave their heavy skirts to drag along in the thick mud. Well-to-do bystanders and passers-by were sickened and appalled by the plight of these poor women as they marched on regardless of the conditions.

When the women at last arrived at Whitehall, caked in mud and exhausted, a small group of them broke off from the main procession and as a deputation went to appeal to Arthur Balfour, the Prime Minister. The women were accompanied by Will and Lansbury, the latter who had organised most of the march.

"What can I do for you?" asked the Prime Minister.
Lansbury stepped forward and spoke on behalf of the deputation. "Mr. Balfour, these good women along with thousands of others have marched here today from places such as Poplar, Edmonton, Paddington, West Ham, Woolwich and Southwark to back up their demands for help for their unemployed men folk." Lansbury beckoned for one of the women to step forward and give her speech, which they had earlier planned, but the poor woman was overcome and broke down. Elizabeth, however, was on hand; she stepped forward and put her arm comfortingly around the sobbing woman.

"Nevermind dearie," she said kindly. She turned to Mr. Balfour, her arm still around the shoulder of the distressed woman. "Mr. Balfour, we've marched all this way because the poor wives of the unemployed cannot suffer in silence any longer. They have been driven here today dragging themselves and their children through the muddy streets to drive home the message that their lot is one of misery, degradation and desperation. Their families are all but starving. We need the Government to help them. The Government has gone to the aid of the tenantry of Ireland, well we're here to tell you that the plight of the poor in London is worse. If this country was threatened with war, the Government would soon find ways to raise money to meet the threat, but Mr. Balfour, the country is faced with a worse evil in the presence of its starving citizens. Please Mr. Balfour, we're pleading with you not to send us away empty handed."

Mr. Balfour listened patiently and then said, "Believe me when I say that I'm sympathetic to your calls, but I see no hope of Parliament voting money in. I'm afraid there's nothing I can do at this time." The deputation left with nothing. The women walked back home in silence and despair.

51

November 14th, 1905

A week after the march as Will and Elizabeth sat subdued eating their breakfast on a Tuesday morning, they were disturbed by a loud, urgent knocking on their street door. Startled, Elizabeth asked, "What on earth is that all about?" They were used to the constant knocks on the door at all hours from people needing Will's attention for one thing or another, but the urgency of these knocks was something quite different.

"We'll soon find out," said Will as he put down his tea, stood and headed for the door, closely followed by Elizabeth. When he opened the door, one of their neighbours, a friend of Elizabeth's and a wife of one of the unemployed that had also been on the march the week previously waved a newspaper excitedly at them.

"Have you seen the paper?" she squealed excitedly. "Queen Alexandra has made an appeal!"

When she saw the puzzled looks on Will's and Elizabeth's faces she said, "Listen!" and then began to read from the newspaper in her hands. "I appeal to all charitably disposed people in the empire, both men and women, to assist me in alleviating the suffering of the poor starving unemployed during this winter. For this purpose I head the list with £2000."

"That's wonderful!" cried Elizabeth as she threw her arms around her friend and hugged her.

"Indeed it is!" laughed Will. "God save the Queen! Hopefully we'll have many more that will follow her lead."

"Oh I'm sure we will!" said the neighbour. "Now that the Queen has made an appeal we'll get some help at last, just you wait and see."

Their hopes were indeed realised; the King himself then followed his Queen's lead and donated 2000 Guineas; the Prince of Wales £1000 and by the end of that winter the public had followed suit and given £150,000, which proved to be enough for the Distress Committees in London and elsewhere to meet the needs of the unemployed.

52

In December, 1905, Conservative Prime Minister Arthur Balfour resigned and as a result a General Election was called. The election was to take place over the time period of January 12th to February 8th, 1906. Unlike the by-election of 1903 when Will only had three weeks to prepare his campaign; this time he had time to prepare properly. On this occasion he would have to stand against Conservative candidate and Boer War veteran, William Augustus Adam. When the voting was over and the votes were counted, the results were:

William Augustus Adam, Conservative = 6914 votes.
Will Crooks, Labour = 9026 votes.

Will was returned again as the Member of Parliament for Woolwich with a majority of over 2000 votes. Although the excitement of this victory didn't quite match that of the unexpectedness of the win in 1903, it was none the less impressive. It wasn't just Will that had time to properly prepare for the election this time. The Labour Representation Committee also had its first real chance to prepare its candidates and to organize an election campaign. Now the question was, could they better their tally of two seats from the last General Election in 1900.

The answer was, yes, they could. This time 29 successful Labour representatives were elected to Parliament. The Liberals won the election with a landslide victory of 125 seats over all other parties.

Will met with the other 28 elected Labour Representation Committee members for the first time after the election on February 15th. At the meeting, Keir Hardie was elected Chairman, in effect the new Labour leader. Will and his new parliamentary colleagues also decided on a new name for their group, 'The Parliamentary Labour Party'. The Labour Party had officially been born.

Humanising the Poor Law in Poplar and improving the lives of so many was always going to come at a cost, but the improvements were made for humanitarian reasons and not financial ones. Whilst the poor people of Poplar benefited from the reforms, the unscrupulous, such as the slum landlords, the employers of the sweatshops that were forced to treat their employees better, and the contractors that had lost their lucrative contracts gained under the old regime, all held grudges against the Labour men. The aggrieved came together and formed the Poplar Municipal Alliance. They contacted the Local Government Board and made all sorts of claims of wrong doing and extravagance against the Guardians. The Press, especially the section that held more conservative views, were all too happy to run sensationalised headlines regarding the Municipal Alliance's charges.

The Guardians, with nothing to hide invited a public Inquiry. The Local Government Board decided that it would indeed conduct such an Inquiry. The Guardians instructed their officers to assist in the Inquiry in any way they could. However, the Local Government Board decided to hold a preliminary Inquiry away from the public gaze and the Guardians were not at all happy with the way it was carried out. It became obvious early on to the Guardians that the Government Board was being used as a tool by the Municipal Alliance. From the onset the Guardians believed that the actions taken by the board in this initial investigation were the actions of a board that already believed the Guardians were guilty of something; they just didn't know what. The Guardians felt the Government Board were obviously hoping that the initial investigation would turn up some type of evidence of wrong doing, but it did not. The fact that the Inquiry was to be conducted by Mr. J. S. Davy, a Government Inspector already known to be against Poplar Poor Law policy only went to prove to the Guardians that the Local Government Board had already decided Poplar's guilt. Will even went as far as to raise this concern over Mr. Davy's suitability because of his already expressed opinions of the Poplar Guardians in Parliament before the Inquiry began, but his concerns were ignored.

On Thursday, June 7th, 1906, the first day of the public Inquiry, Will and his fellow Guardians again protested strongly that it was to be held by an individual that they felt had already made up his mind as to their guilt. They expressed their concern that it would be quite unjust to appoint so extreme an opponent of their policy to conduct the Inquiry. In his opening speech to the Inquiry, Will told the Inspector, "I want to say that we welcome this public Inquiry. There is only one small anxiety, and that is that we think we should have had some person to conduct the proceedings who has not already expressed an opinion with regard to our conduct. Naturally we are somewhat anxious about that. We hope, however, that the spirit of fair-play which is so predominant in all Englishmen and the English character will cause you to dismiss from your mind any impressions you may have had, and that you will hear the evidence impartially which may be set before you."

The Guardians having nothing to hide decided to defend themselves at the Inquiry, with Will in his role as Chairman representing them, however, when it became obvious in the early days of the proceedings that the Local Government Board were letting the Municipal Alliance run the Inquiry, the Guardians took the decision to call in legal representation in the form of Mr. Corrie Grant. Mr. Grant's first utterance at the Inquiry was to complain that the Local Government Board, while seemingly allowing the Municipal Alliance free reign, had put obstacles in the way of his obtaining necessary information relating to the Inquiry.

As the Inquiry progressed, witness after witness was brought forward by the Alliance, but not one charge was backed up or proven. The Local Government Board did nothing to try to stop the Press from printing these unsubstantiated charges and they had a field day with headlines such as 'Luxuries for Paupers', 'A Pauper paradise' and 'High life in the Poplar workhouse' dominating the newspaper stands. Because the Poplar Board of Guardians were led by well-known Labour men such as Will and Lansbury, the public were encouraged to believe that the board's policy was what happens in a Labour run administration. However, the truth is that out of the 24 members of the board, only 10 of them were Labour representatives. The majority of the Guardians on the board were in fact Conservatives and Liberals. Day after day during the Inquiry the sensational allegations continued where they promptly appeared as the next day's newspaper headlines, and day after day, Will appealed for the proof of fraud or corruption, but still none came. The Inquiry ran for 20 days.

Shortly after the Inquiry had finished, the Local Government Board released its report. It was damning! In response, Will took pen to paper and wrote an open letter to the Press. He wrote:

"Let me begin by saying that the unfairness and injustice of the report are so far recognised that today I have been told by members of all parties that the report is not only wicked, but brutal. Will you permit me to make it public through your columns that I accept the challenge thrown down in the Local Government Board report? Against all its strictures I intend to maintain my stand on that policy of humanising the Poor Law to which I have given the greater part of my life and in doing so I propose to appeal from the Local Government Board to the public.

If the public upholds this insult to the poor I shall be painfully surprised. After 20 days of a searching Inquiry, and after twice 20 pages of a strained attack on Mr. Lansbury and myself, there is nothing to show that we have done anything against the actual orders and regulations of the very board that now rises in mock-heroic wrath to slay us. Our only crime is that we have humanised a system framed in 1834, when the voteless working classes were dragooned by a middle-class majority.

In our efforts as Labour men to humanise this system we had to some extent the co-operation of Conservative Ministers. Witness Mr. Chaplin's circular on the need for adequate out-relief, and Mr. Long's and Mr. Balfour's efforts for the Unemployed Bill. When distress was at its height we saw our policy nobly supported by the highest lady in the land. In response to Queen Alexandra's appeal the British public subscribed £150,000 for the very class who are insulted in this report. Now that we have had a change in the political parties, one of the first things the new Government does is to subject that policy to an underhanded attack.

That makes my present duty clear. The public may remember that at Mr. Chaplin's request I went as a nominee of the Local Government Board on the Metropolitan Asylums Board. It may remember that I was co-opted on the Central Unemployed Body on the suggestion of Mr. Walter Long. Now that the Local Government Board, under the new Government, has seen fit to attack me and my Labour colleagues, and to flout the poor as I venture to say they have never been flouted by that department before, I can no longer hold those two positions. I propose to resign. Nor until its attitude towards the poor and the unemployed changes will I ever consent to represent the Local Government Board on any public body again. I prefer to represent the people.

The fight on this new policy for the aged poor and the unemployed will be a long one. I may not live to see the end. But I say now what I told the Inspector at the Inquiry, that black though Poplar has been made to appear, the time will come when it will stand out as a shining light. As it stands, the report is an attempt to intimidate a democratically elected Board of Guardians. Until we are dismissed or imprisoned, the Poplar Board of Guardians, backed, as I know we shall be, by the electors, intend to go on carrying out the humane system we inaugurated; a system which Mr. Chaplin recommended as a model to the unions of the country. The faults of administration, so grossly magnified in this report, are common to all such bodies, and Poplar will do its best to avoid them. But the policy will not change. By that we stand or fall."

54

On the heels of the damning Local Government report, Will did in fact receive some good news. The new Liberal Government that was elected into power earlier in the year, renewed the Unemployed Workmen Act from the previous year and voted £200,000 into the Distress Committees fund, which saw the State prepare to meet the needs of the unemployed in the coming winter. Unemployment was now a national responsibility. Will, along with the women of the unemployed that had marched to Whitehall, had at last seen their efforts rewarded.

A Sunday Morning, June, 1906

Will's first scheduled public appearance after the end of the Inquiry just happened to be at his College at the dock gates. Would the people of Poplar have had their minds turned against him by the misinformation spread by the London Press and the Municipal Alliance, or did they know him so well as not to be swayed by the personal attacks the Press had made against his character?

If he had any worries about a public backlash to the negative press they quickly vanished as he approached the dock gates. Ahead of him swelled one of the largest crowds that he had ever had at one of his Colleges, as thousands of Poplar ratepayers gathered there to show their support.

"Here he comes!" shouted one of the men in the crowd as he saw Will approach.

As the crowd parted to let him pass through so that he could get to his portable rostrum, they erupted into a chorus of cheers and applause. Men slapped him across his back. "We're with you, Will!" they told him. "The papers don't understand Will, they've never been poor and gone through what we have," another called.

"They haven't got a clue!" shouted another as Will passed by.

When he finally made his way through the throng of well-wishers and reached the rostrum, the cheering and applause was still going strong. He climbed up onto the rostrum and gestured with his outstretched hands for everybody to settle down. When at last they did, his voice cracked a little under the emotion, but he soon recovered and managed to say in his usual loud, clear, deep voice, which always seemed to carry across the whole crowd, "Thank you my dear friends for one of the greatest and emotional receptions of my life." Again the crowd erupted in response.

"The people of Poplar know the truth about the Inquiry; the people of London do not. They only have the Press's version. Let me tell you that I believe in being a true Guardian of the poor, and not merely a Guardian of the Poor Rate. We in Poplar have preferred to save the lives of the poor rather than the rates. Even then we have administered with remarkable economy; for Poplar's rates would not be high if London as a whole paid its proper share towards maintaining London's poor. We in Poplar, however, have not allowed an unjust rating system to prevent us from doing our duty to broken-down old people, to the starving and to the unemployed. We agree with Thomas Carlyle that 'to believe practically, that the poor and luckless are here only as a nuisance to be abraded and abated, and in some permissible manner made away with, and swept out of sight, is not an amiable faith. To say to the poor: Ye shall eat the bread of affliction and drink the water of affliction and be very miserable while here, requires not so much a stretch of heroic faculty in any sense as due toughness of bowels.'

I am sometimes told that I affect to despise my critics. You know better, of course. But really, after such experiences as these, I can't help laughing at them when I think of their ponderous official pronouncements against my policy and of the equally ponderous lectures read to me by certain sections of the Press and the Church. When will the Press and the Church, and 'all who are put in authority over us', come to learn what the mind of the people really is, and begin to interpret it rightly? I know the heart of the people to be true. That is why I laugh and go on my way confident that the little piece of well-doing I have aimed at on behalf of the poor and the unemployed will in the end put to 'silence the ignorance of foolish men.'

Give us the same terrible state of things that we had in some of the previous winters, and I shall apply the same remedy again. The law is there for the sake of the poor, not for the sake of officials. My policy is not a haphazard one. It is the outcome of years of experience. It is fundamentally sound, and will one day become a national policy."

1908

Since joining the National Pension Committee back in 1898, Will, like the rest of the committee had worked tirelessly in the fight to secure a national pension scheme in Britain. Their ten year campaign saw some reward in 1908 with the introduction of the 'Old Age Pensions Bill', which was currently being debated in Parliament. Once introduced, a Bill must go through a number of stages before it can become law as an Act, as this allows the Bill's provisions to be debated, and for amendments to the original Bill to also be introduced, debated, and agreed to.

However, although a pensions Bill was welcomed, it was received with mixed emotions. For Will and the likes of George Lansbury and Keir Hardie, the Bill came with too many conditions attached. They believed that the Bill should cover everyone over a certain retirement age and not just the people that met the strict criteria laid out in it.

As the Bill stood, a pension would only be paid to people over 70 years of age that were earning less than £21 and 10 shillings per year, and that also passed a strict 'character test'. For these old people of 'good' character, a single person would receive a weekly pension of five shillings per week and married couples would receive seven shillings and sixpence.

On July 9th, 1908, in the House of Commons, Will got to his feet and addressed Parliament on the Pension Bill. He began by saying, "I have read somewhere that life is a comedy to a thinking man and a tragedy to a feeling man. That is all the difference in the world. We have had an exhibition of thinking without feeling. I have felt pretty keenly about the whole business, listening to the flippancy which one expects at some kind of Tory meeting. In a pamphlet which I wrote ten years ago I anticipated that whenever a scheme of old-age pensions was considered in the House of Commons it would be called 'a glorified outdoor relief.' So is every kind of pension that is paid out of the taxpayer's pockets.

We have been told by opponents of the Bill about inquisitorial examinations of claimants for a pension. It is very good of these Honourable Gentlemen, I admit it. Is it not the case that Honourable Gentlemen and Right Honourable Gentlemen who receive pensions from His Majesty's Government are obliged to declare in writing their impecuniosity? How dreadfully lowering and degrading it must be to a man whose private income would be wealth beyond the dreams of avarice to an ordinary poor man in this country! Yet he has the nerve to write to somebody and to declare his impecuniosity before he gets his £1200 a year! No man reads him a little homily on thrift. No man says a word about it. There is nothing degrading about pensions at all, except when they get down to five shillings a week. They are not awfully degrading, but the reward for services to the State; that is if they are anything between £1200 and £4000 a year. They then add to the dignity and importance of His Majesty's subjects.

The noble Lord who spoke earlier in the afternoon made a glaring mistake when he said that no member of a friendly society (workers contributed a small sum to friendly societies as a means of reducing their chances of ending their days in the workhouse because of a lack of money in their old age) ended up in the workhouse, because a report was produced in 1901 by the Charity Organisation Society showing the number of members of friendly societies who were in the workhouse. This report shows that there were in fact 4000 men in the workhouses of England and Wales who had been members of friendly societies for thirty years and upwards. I do not take my own figures in this matter.

It is an astonishing thing that facts like these have been the excuse for not providing pensions earlier. Nothing was done by the Unionist Party in 1899 because the cost of the aged poor had been captured by Charity Organisations and through the Poor Law. Then they gave several homilies on the Poor Law Act of 1834, but if they had kept up to date with regard to that Act they would have found that with rules and regulations that had been made since, there is hardly a vestige of the 1834 Act left.

There is a Poor Law Commission sitting now, (members opposing the Bill wanted to wait for the results from the Commission which was set up by the previous government before considering a pension Bill. However, the Commission had already been sitting for three years) and that would be a reason for doing nothing, because whenever the late Government wished to do nothing they appointed a Royal Commission. Let me illustrate the case of the man who once saw a lot of coloured cooked eggs on a barrow, and he said, 'What are those eggs, guvnor?'

'Oh, they are partridge eggs.'

'Do you think a hen would bring them off?'

'Yes, I should think so.'

'Then how much for a sitting?'

'A shilling and a share of your luck.'

About four weeks after he turned up again and gazed wistfully at the stall. The stall-holder recognised him and asked, 'Well, what luck?'

'Oh, you never saw anything like it in your life. That hen, she sat and sat, and I'm blowed if she didn't cook them.'

Well I tell you gentlemen that there has never been an Old-Age Pension Commission or a Poor Law Commission which did not well cook their

Reports before bringing them to this House." This brought laughter from the benches and Will continued.

"The regulations of the Board have amended Poor Law relief out of all knowledge. They told us to give outdoor relief generously, and in giving it to old and deserving people we should not rake up the past. I was a Guardian and I wished to do it generously. Some said, "They do not want old-age pensions; you want to make the workhouse more comfortable." Well we did that, and what was the result? I was put on trial and very nearly got time.

I rejoice at the start that is now going to be made. I do not contend for a moment that the leader of the opposition was not right when he said you will not get rid of a certain class of people; but what I am afraid of is, and I hope those who draw up these regulations will bear this in mind, that if charity commissioners and Boards of Guardians are connected with it, you must safeguard people who require infirmity relief from being pushed into some dark squalid hole and left there. There are many people who if they had £1 a week could not take care of themselves. This Bill is not wanted for that purpose; it is wanted for people who can look after themselves. I believe it will stop the recruiting for the workhouse. God knows what sacrifices are made by children to keep their parents and little children to keep their grandparents. I know a man who had to go to his old mother and say: 'These are the boots off my children, mother; what am I to do?' And the old mother, out of her love for the little ones, made the plunge and went into the workhouse in order to keep the boots on the feet of the little children. In this case we know what we want, and we do not want it to be said hereafter that when this Bill was before the House we said we would rest content with this. We are going to prevent old folk breaking up their homes. They struggle on to keep a roof over them, and you wonder why they are content to live in misery and squalor when they can go to the workhouse and be well tended. There is one thing the value of which you cannot define and that is liberty. There are none so poor but they would give their lives for it, and what I want to do, and what I am sure we shall do by this Bill, is to enable the children to keep their parents and give them what they cannot buy, a little love and sympathy."

With his hand, Will gestured to the House in general and asked "What have you done all the time? If ever you wanted an objectionable rate or if ever you wanted to get anything that would be fought against, you put it on to the poor rate. Thus it was made to appear that you were spending millions and millions on the poor, when you were doing nothing of the kind. What are the actual figures? In 1905-6, there was roughly £30,000,000 collected in England and Wales under the head of the Poor

Law, or £26,000,000 in England and Wales excluding London; but the actual amount paid in indoor and outdoor relief was £6,603,549.

Why deceive the public to this extent? Why do you not tell the truth about the figures? There are just under 300,000 aged people, or perhaps a few more, who are getting indoor or outdoor relief, and there are very nearly 600,000 who do not get any relief at all. That shows that two persons out of every three manage to keep out of the workhouse somehow.

It is wonderful what we have heard in this House that people can do when they are seventy. It is a revelation! The Right Honourable Gentleman has just talked about a man going to work and of subsidising his employer. I know, as a Poor Law Guardian and an administrator, that many and many a sweater has taken account of a poor wretched woman's two shillings and sixpence which the Guardians have allowed her to help her to pay her rent, and has reduced the price for shirt-making in consequence of that outdoor relief. Yet the moment you attempt to lift people up and make men and women of them, it is almost a criminal offence." He shook his head in disappointment before carrying on.

"We may surely call these old-age pensions, very old-age pensions. I wonder any Member has the temerity to get up in this House and object to them. I once said, and I repeat, that no man should sit in this House without having served first for ten years as a Poor Law Guardian. He would then know something about human nature. It is not perfect. There are a good many sides to it, but most people who apply for relief are very human, and I do not think they very much object to these inquisitorial examinations as to their character.

We were challenged by the Honourable Member for Preston, who said, 'Would you go on any public platform and declare that you are in favour of giving a pension of five shillings per week to a drunken, thriftless, worthless man or woman?' My reply is very prompt to that. A man of seventy with nothing in the world to help him is going to cut a pretty shine on five shillings per week, whether his character be good or bad. What could he do with it? It is not enough to keep him in decency, and he would be well punished for not taking care when he had the opportunity if he had to live on five shillings per week."

His tone then changed as a hint of anger rose up in him. "Who are you, to be continually finding fault? Who amongst you has such a clear record as to be able to point to the iniquity and wickedness of an old man of seventy? I said before, and I repeat, if a man is foolish enough to get old, and if he has not been artful enough to get rich, you have no right to punish him for it. It is no business of yours. It is sufficient for you to know he has grown old. After all, who are these old men and women? They are the veterans of industry, people of almost endless toil, who have fought for and won the industrial and commercial supremacy of Great Britain. Is it their lot and end to be the bastille of the everlasting slur of pauperism? We claim these pensions as a right. Ruskin, I think, read you a little homily on the subject:

'Even a labourer serves his country with his spade and shovel as the statesman does with his pen or the soldier with his sword.'

He has a right to some consideration from the State. Here in a country rich beyond description there are people poor beyond description. There can be no earthly excuse for the condition of things which exists in this country today. If it be necessary to have a strong Army and Navy to protect the wealth of the nation, do not let us forget that it is the veterans of industry who have created that wealth. Let us accept this as an installment to bring decency and comfort to our aged men and women."

The Bill passed, and on August 1st, 1908, the Liberal government introduced the Old Age Pensions Act. Although the Act still came with the limitations as outlined in the Bill, in that it would only be paid to people over 70 years of age that met all the strict conditions laid out in it, it was nonetheless a giant step in the right direction.

1910

In November, 1909, David Lloyd George, the Chancellor of the Exchequer in Herbert Asquith's Liberal government declared war on poverty and squalidness. His 'people's budget' was to be paid for by taxing the rich and the landed gentry. The House of Lords, however, packed as it was with the rich and landed gentry threw out the budget on November 30th and as a result a general election was called for January, 1910.

Unfortunately for Will, when news reached him of the election he was actually in Australia. He had sailed to Canada in September with Elizabeth before then sailing on to Australia. Plans had already been made to visit New Zealand after the Australian leg of their trip came to an end. The trip was a mix of pleasure; the recharging of his batteries after another bout of ill health; a hope to learn something of the spirit of the people from the colonies; a firsthand look at what the social conditions of the colonies were like, and a wish to connect with his Labour colleagues in the colonies. Will and the Labour men involved in the great dock strike of 1889 had not forgotten the help they had received from the colonies, especially Australia who had sent £30,000 to help the dock workers when it was most needed.

Will carried with him the message from the Labour movement that 'Solidarity of Labour is the hope of the world'. Because of the arrangements that had already been made for meetings and his public appearances (appearances that were packing the halls where they were held), and of course the length and the time of the journey home, (the average time for a mail steamer journey from Australia to England took 40 days), Will didn't even know if he would be home before the Polls closed, let alone be there to campaign to defend his seat. Of course he was still going to defend it, but it fell to his election agent and team back home to run his campaign in his absence.

His tour of the colonies had been a great success, but as he left New Zealand, he stood on the deck of the mail steamer that would be his home for the next 40 days or so and looked out at the vast ocean in front of him and realised that he couldn't wait to get back home to England.

When they did arrive home it was the day before the close of the Polls, so he didn't have to wait long to hear the result from Woolwich.

Will had polled 8420 votes.
His rival polled 8715 votes.

By less than 300 votes, Will had lost his seat and the new Member of Parliament for Woolwich was the Conservative candidate, William Augustus Adam.

Back at home in Gough Street, Elizabeth slumped down into her armchair and asked Will with her voice full of sadness, "What will you do now? The chances are there won't be another election for five years or so."

Will sat down next to her and pointed to the large pile of paperwork and letters piled high on the table that was also his desk. "I have what seems like thousands of requests for public appearances. That will keep me occupied for quite some time I should think. Keep your spirits up, love, we only lost by less than 300 Votes. I'm sure we can turn that around at the next election, whenever that will be."

58

December, 1910

Elizabeth heard Will enter the house and called from the kitchen, "Hello love, I'm in the kitchen just brewing some tea. Can I get you some?"

"Yes please, love," he called back as he made his way into the kitchen to join her. When he entered the kitchen he was grinning broadly.

"What are you grinning at?" she asked.

"There's going to be a general election," Will said, beaming.
Elizabeth's face dropped. "Oh Will," she said. "Come and sit down." She took his hand and led him to the kitchen table where she made him sit down. The grin had now left Will's face and was replaced by a look of total confusion.

"What's wrong?" he asked, now looking concerned as he sat down.
Elizabeth pulled a chair out from under the table and placed it in front of Will so they were facing each other. She sat down and took Will's hands in hers and then she began rubbing them tenderly trying to soothe him; her nurse's instincts guiding her. She looked into his eyes, concern written across her face. Speaking very clearly, she said gently. "Will, the general election has already taken place. It happened just a few months ago. You're getting confused. Try to think back and remember. It took place earlier in the year, just after our trip abroad." They sat in silence for a few seconds with Will looking totally confused, but then at last he roared with laughter.

"What's wrong?" asked Elizabeth, looking even more concerned now, and wondering if she should call for the doctor.

At last, Will settled down. "You foolish woman!" he laughed. "There's going to be 'another' general election in December. The hung Parliament just isn't working, so Asquith wants to go back to the people and has called another general election."

"Oh," said Elizabeth, somewhat sheepishly and then asked, "Has there ever been two elections in one year before?"

"Not that I know of. I believe this will be the first time ever," he replied. Will then grinned at Elizabeth and said, "So you thought I was losing my mind did you?"

"Oh Will, I'm sorry, I feel so silly." But this time they both roared with laughter.

Will was a long way from losing his mind; in fact, after his long trip to the colonies and his break from the House of Commons he was ready for the fight ahead. He had only narrowly lost his Woolwich seat earlier in the year, so he knew he had a good chance of winning it back and he was soon out on the streets of Woolwich and filling the halls again campaigning.

As the election date approached, it was clear that the fight for Woolwich was still going to be a close one. Opinion seemed to be split rather evenly between Will and his conservative rival, William Augustus Adam, and so on a chilly December evening, Will and Elizabeth stood in the Town Hall waiting for the results to be announced. Amid the building tension, the returning officer announced the result. "Here are the results for the constituency of Woolwich!

    William Augustus Adam. Conservative = 8016 votes.
    Will Crooks. Labour = 8252 votes."

This time it was Will that had won by less than 300 votes. The Labour supporters in the hall erupted and through the noise the returning officer called, "Will Crooks is duly elected the Member of Parliament for Woolwich." He was one of 42 Labour MPs elected.

1912

Will had just left a meeting at the Guildhall in central London. The Guildhall is a medieval Grade I listed landmark building that has stood for over five hundred years and has been a center for City power since the days when the Lord Mayor of London's influence almost matched that of the Monarch.

Will was running a little late for another meeting as he rushed through the Guildhall struggling to close his bulging leather briefcase as he headed for the exit. Not looking where he was going, he bumped heavily into another man who was entering the building.

"I'm dreadfully sorry," Will apologised, and then as he recognised the man added, "Goodness me, Reverend Stead! How on earth are you? It's been quite a while since our paths have crossed," and he shook the Reverend's hand vigorously. Will of course knew the Reverend Francis Herbert Stead from the Committee that campaigned for a National Old Age Pension. He had been responsible for getting the campaign started after he had arranged the initial meetings at the Browning Hall settlement in Walworth.

Reverend Stead smiled at seeing Will, even though he had just almost been knocked off his feet by him. "It has indeed been a while, Will, and I see in the newspapers that you continue to do great work," but his smile quickly faded, "but I'm afraid things haven't been very good for me recently."

"I'm sorry to hear that, old chap. Is it something you can talk about?" asked Will, concerned for his old friend's well-being. The Reverend sighed sadly and said, "You remember my brother, William, don't you Will? I believe we've spoken of him in the past."

"Of course I do," confirmed Will. "I've met William on a number of occasions. He's a first class investigative journalist."

"He 'was' a first class journalist," the Reverend corrected him. "I'm afraid he died recently in somewhat unpleasant circumstances."

"Oh my dear Reverend, I'm so sorry to hear that. What on earth happened?"

Reverend Stead took a deep breath and said sadly, "William was asked to speak at an international conference on world peace at Carnegie Hall, in New York. He was traveling there when he died. He was a passenger on the Titanic."

60

Under the 'Acts of Union of 1800', the Kingdoms of Great Britain and Ireland were joined and became the 'United Kingdom of Great Britain and Ireland', in effect making Ireland part of the British state.

However, from around 1885, Home Rule for Ireland came to dominate domestic British politics. Irish Home Rule would free Ireland from the direct rule of London and appease those who wanted more power for the Irish to govern themselves. Home Rule for Ireland was something that the Liberal Government of Herbert Asquith were strongly in favour of, although not all Liberals shared this view. Indeed, there was such fierce opposition to Irish Home Rule from within the Liberal party itself that in 1886 a group of Liberal MPs actually split away from the main party to become the 'Liberal Unionists' because they believed so strongly in the preservation of the British-Irish union.

They were not the only ones to object to Asquith's plans for Irish Home Rule. An assortment of parties that were against the Bill came together under a Unionist banner. These Unionists vigorously opposed the Bill as they saw it as the beginning of the break-up of the Empire. The Unionists were dominated by the Conservative Party, which had recently merged with the Liberal Unionists and had now adopted the title of the Conservative and Unionist Party, although that title is now rarely used and the party is now commonly referred to as just the 'Conservative party'.

November 12th, 1912. House of Commons

A Unionist, Conservative member Sir Frederick Banbury, unexpectedly introduced an amendment to the Irish Home Rule Bill, which would drastically cut the amount of money that was to be transferred to the new Irish Government. Many members that supported the Home Rule Bill were away from the House not expecting important business to come up that day and this was what the Unionists were hoping for. They turned up in force to vote on this last minute amendment knowing they would have the majority in the House that day. The Unionist plan worked and they won the vote by 22 votes, thus carrying the amendment. The Liberal Government and their allies, including the Labour Party were furious at what they saw as underhanded tactics by the opposition. The victorious Unionists, however, taunted the Government and the Prime Minister, Mr. Asquith with cries of 'Resign' and 'Dissolve'. Under the circumstances of the vote, with the House being so light with many Government members not present for the vote, the Government did not see the loss as a vote of confidence and had no intention of resigning; in fact, the next day on November 13th,

Prime Minister Asquith moved to rescind the amendment. The Speaker told Mr. Asquith that he could find no precedent for rescinding a decision of the House that had been arrived at in discussion of a Bill.

When Sir Rufus Isaacs, the Attorney General rose on behalf of the Government and tried to debate the subject, the Unionists shouted him down. Every time Sir Rufus and his colleagues tried to speak, the Unionists hurled derisive remarks at them, making it impossible for anyone to be heard. The speaker, Mr. Lowther, at last adjourned the House for one hour to give everyone a chance to calm down.

After one hour the members filed back into the chamber, but again when anyone from the Government tried to speak he was met by cries of derision from the Unionist benches. The speaker tried desperately to restore order, but after many attempts he had no choice but to adjoin the House until the next day. The Unionists took this as a huge victory for their obstructive tactics and taunted the Government even further with cries of 'Traitors' and 'Resign'. In the heat of the moment the excited Unionists lost their heads somewhat and began throwing pamphlets and Government reports at Mr. Asquith and his colleagues. Outraged, the Liberal benches rushed forward towards the Unionist benches and in return the Unionist benches rushed back across the house to meet them with lots of pushing and gesturing from both sides. Tempers flared and it seemed it was just a matter of time before punches were thrown. One of the Unionist members seized the Speaker's copy of the Standing Orders book and threw it angrily across the House, striking Winston Churchill, now a Liberal and First Lord of the Admiralty full in the face. Churchill's eyes widened in anger and his nostrils flared as he sought out the Unionist that had thrown it. His colleagues sensing that Winston with his fiery temperament and military background could be the first one to actually strike somebody tried desperately to hold him back. The House seemed ready to erupt in violence and get completely out of control, but then above the furor of the angry crowd, a deep voice began to sing out. "Should old acquaintance be forgot and never brought to mind, should old acquaintance be forgot and old lang syne."

All heads turned towards the Labour benches, where Will, his deep voice bellowing out was singing loudly. The other members that had been trying to keep the peace quickly followed his lead and joined him in song by singing, "For auld lang syne, my dear, for auld lang syne." The angry members that had just been ready to fight each other, now actually began to laugh at the absurdness of the situation and a semblance of order returned to the House. Violence had been averted. Members from both sides slowly regained their composure and departed the House peacefully, not quite believing the bizarre scenes that they had just witnessed.

1913

Will was often at his happiest when he was out and about walking the streets of the East End and Woolwich where he could stop and chat to his fellow east enders and constituents. Always approachable and always ready to share a story and a joke, this was where his soul felt nourished. This is also where he found his energy and his inspiration to continue the fight for the rights of the working man.

Today as he walked along enjoying his stroll, the smell of freshly baked bread drew his attention to the bakers shop where a thin, harried looking middle aged woman was just exiting. Will recognised the woman. "Hello Mrs. Clark, how's your husband these days? The last time I saw him he was still looking for work."

"Oh hello, Mr. Crooks," she replied rather sadly. "He's working now for what it's worth, but he's only earning 26 shillings a week. I'm grateful he's in work, Mr. Crooks, truly I am, but it's so hard to get through the week on that kind of money. I often go without at the end of the week so he and the children get to eat, but like I say, I'm just grateful he's got work." Will felt the flame of anger burn inside of him. "I'm so sorry," he said. "You're not the only wife that I've spoken to today that has complained of their husband's low pay."

April 10th, 1913. House of Commons

In Parliament, Will put forward a resolution calling for a minimum wage. He stood and addressed the House. "I put forward this resolution calling for a minimum wage because the right of every family in the country to an income sufficient to enable it to maintain its members in decency and comfort should be recognised, and this House should therefore be of the opinion that the Trade Boards Act should be so extended as to provide for the establishment of a minimum wage of at least 30 shillings per week for every adult worker in urban areas and a minimum wage that will secure an approximately equal standard of life for every adult worker in rural areas; and this House also declares that the Government should set an example by adopting the minimum wage of 30 shillings per week in its own workshops and insert it as a condition in all contracts.

I call for the House to welcome the setting up of any effective machinery whereby a legal minimum wage might be secured to the worker in all those trades in which wages are below subsistence point and is of the opinion that a minimum standard of living cannot be secured for the whole community apart from such enactment.

Let me tell you gentlemen that I myself have worked for 30 shillings a week, as I have for less than 30 shillings a week, but I have never worked for less than 30 shillings without getting into debt.

Decency and comfort!" cried Will, his voice thundering across the House. "Is there any man in this House who can define decency and comfort? You could not get decency and comfort for three times 30 shillings a week.

I have known Government employees on leaving home on Friday morning to go to work stopped by their wives with the cry 'Don't be late home; you're taking the last bit of bread and we shall have none until you come home.'

Don't you feel ashamed of yourselves?" cried Will. "Why if the Empire was in danger from invasion, all the millions of money necessary for its defence would be found. Don't you see that in feeding the people properly you are strengthening the Empire?"

Will threw out his hands imploring the Government. "I want you to give every man something to live for. We ask for him a man's share of the produce of his industry; not a dog's share; not a horse's share; not a pig's share, but a man's share. You cannot deny it to him. You must afford it, or someday the working men will make you."

---

86 years later on April 1st, 1999, Tony Blair's Labour Government finally introduced Britain's first ever Minimum Wage.

1914

War had broken out in Europe. When Germany declared war on France and the German troops poured into Belgium as a way of reaching France, the British foreign secretary, Sir Edward Grey, sent an ultimatum to Germany demanding their withdrawal from the neutral Belgium. When Germany did not withdraw, Britain declared war on Germany.

Before this war, Will had always been strongly opposed to conflict. He was a very outspoken critic during the Boer war, which he viewed as unjust in that the Government of the day were fighting to expand the Empire and federating South Africa under the British flag. The war with Germany, however, was seen as a direct threat to the British Isles themselves as the conflict involved Britain's closest neighbour, France. If the Germans were victorious in France, then they would only be across the channel and the threat of invasion was very real. For Will, this war was not a Government war, but a people's war.

He felt so strongly about the just cause of the war that he became a leading recruiter for the war effort and travelled thousands of miles speaking to men of all classes in the hope of persuading them to enlist. He also visited the front on many occasions carrying messages of encouragement and the good wishes from the British people.

Down at the dock gates, he told his College, "I was strongly anti-war before this war began. I was so strongly for peace that I was willing to fight any man for it. Although my party's leader, Ramsay MacDonald, felt compelled to resign his leadership because we as a parliamentary party decided to back the Government on this war, I myself again state that I am 100 percent with the Government on this. My conscience compels it. I tell you all that you and I have got to shoulder our burden in these demanding times. We have got to see the old country through, and stand shoulder to shoulder to present a united front to the enemy.

It fills my heart with pride when I see so many of our local men enlisting to sign up and protect us all, but of course it also breaks my heart to see so many of them killed or injured in the trenches. They realise that our homes are in danger and that our wives and families are threatened. The brutal murders of innocent folk in Belgium show us what Germany would do if they reached these shores. Our men are fighting for liberty and for our homes. Let me tell you a story; I was walking down Commercial Road with a young fellow dressed in his khaki uniform, fresh back from the front

Where there's a Will, there's a way

when he saw an old mate in the street. 'Why, Bert', he said, 'Not in khaki? You've not joined up then?'

'Naw!' Bert replied. 'I'm not a fool'. And then he began to argue against the war. The soldier had to leave, but I remained and turned to the young fellow. I purposely raised my voice to attract the attention of passers-by.

'Do you understand that it is the likes of him, doing what he is doing, that enables the likes of you to be where you are in safety. You are not willing to do your bit to stop the Kaiser from murdering women and children.' By this time a large number of women were standing around listening. 'Let me tell you about a scene at a Belgian railway station a little while ago,' I said.

'A train was loaded up with 800 young women; married and single. They had been dragged from their homes by the German soldiers. Tears were on their faces, and their hands were outstretched as they cried, 'Where are we going? For God's sake, tell us where we are going!' They were being dragged from their homes to Germany. And you my lad, are not such a fool, you say, as to help to save your women and children from a fate like this.' There was no need for me to say any more. I heard the women calling, 'Leave him to us, Mr. Crooks, leave him to us.' So I left." His audience gave a hearty round of applause at this and when they had finished, he added:

"Well that is how our women feel about it all. They encourage their loved ones to go and fight. They want this dreadful war to be over, but they do not want it to be over until the power of the Kaiser to repeat such evil has been broken."

63

It was a new year; 1916. Will rubbed his hands together to warm them as he looked out of the window onto Gough Street. There had been a light sprinkling of snow, the second flurry that morning, but it showed no sign of settling. He turned, walked over to the fireplace and placed one hand on the mantelpiece to steady himself as he leant forward to place a few more pieces of coal onto the fire, which he had taken from the iron coal bucket sitting on the small hearth. He then took the poker that stood next to the bucket and poked it into the fire to coax it into more life.

"That's nice, Will," Elizabeth told him. "I was just starting to feel chilled."

"There's another little flurry outside, but it doesn't look like it'll settle," Will told her.

Elizabeth was sat at the large table that was littered with documents and letters. She was working her way through opening the morning's mail and arranging it so that it was easier for Will to process. Will joined her at the table and sat across from her. He picked up some of the letters that she had already opened and sorted for him and started reading. She soon interrupted him, however, as one of the letters clearly had her perplexed.

"Will?" she asked. "What does P.C. mean?"

"P.C.?" he repeated. "I assume it means Privy Counsellor, as in 'Privy Counsellor' to the monarch. Who's the letter from? Does it have P.C. after their name?" Elizabeth didn't answer. She just dissolved into tears.

"What on earth's wrong?" Will asked as he stood up again and walked around the table and took the letter from her. As he read it, he soon realised that the P.C. did indeed stand for what he thought it did. The letter was informing him that he was being invited to be one of King George V's Privy Counsellors. When Elizabeth had regained her composure, she asked, "Do you know exactly what being a Privy Counsellor involves?"

Will put on a posh voice and said, "I believe the Privy Council usually meets around once a month, usually where the monarch is residing and advises the King on the exercise of royal prerogative, my good woman." Elizabeth laughed. "Well, well, fancy that, Will."

"I know," said Will, turning serious. "What an honour. Who would have thought that a working class Poplar boy would ever be made Privy Counsellor to the King."

On the morning of January 27th, 1916, Elizabeth fussed over Will's appearance before she let him leave the house.

"I'm fine!" he protested as she straightened his tie for the third time. She had already made sure there wasn't a hair on his head out of place; that his greying beard was neatly trimmed and that his black shoes were finely polished.

"I'll tell you when you're fine!" she scolded. "This is a big day, Will. You're going to the Palace. You'll be seeing the King."

"Stop fretting woman, I've seen the King on numerous occasions and he me."

"Yes, but today you're going to see him at home, in the Palace."

Will just sighed and let her fuss over him until she was satisfied. When she was, she gave him a kiss for good luck and then let him leave.

Later that day at Buckingham Palace, an immaculately turned out Will, by his Majesty's command was sworn in as one of His Majesty, King George V's, most honourable Privy Council.

64

Wednesday, June 13th, 1917, was a beautiful hot summer day. The sun was shining in through the open window of the sitting room at the house in Gough Street and the curtains barely moved as a slight breeze gently caressed them. Will sat quietly in his shirtsleeves with his open case of documents by his side as he sipped from a cup of tea, reading a letter from one of his constituents. It had been a busy morning up until then opening and reading his mail with Elizabeth and then writing a few letters of his own in reply. The ticking of the large clock on the mantelpiece and the occasional rustle of the paper in Will's hand were the only sounds that disturbed the stillness. It was hard to believe there was a war on, but WW1 had been raging now for three long years.

He finished reading the letter and filed it away back in his suitcase. The clock on the mantel showed just after 11.30 a.m. He stood just as Elizabeth came in from the back garden where she had been hanging out some wet clothes on the washing line. She was inspecting some large wooden clothes pegs in her hands for damage before placing them back into her apron pockets. Will pulled his jacket on. "I'll be out for most of the afternoon as I've quite a few people to see," he told Elizabeth.

"All right, Will," she said. "I'll see you later then. I need to scrub the doorstep anyway so it should be nice and dry by the time you get home."

He kissed her goodbye, put on his hat and left the house. He walked along the narrow pavement of Gough Street, into Thomas Street and then turned into Upper North Street. He soon had to pull out his handkerchief and wipe sweat from the back of his neck and from his forehead. He sat down on a nearby low wall at the front of a house and took a few minutes to rest. He was now 65 and he felt his age. His past illnesses had taken their toll on him physically, but that didn't stop him doing what he loved and that was getting out and about among the people of Poplar and Woolwich. Admittedly it took him a lot longer to get anywhere now on foot, but he still preferred that mode of transport for short distances, even though Elizabeth now regularly encouraged him to use the omnibuses more whenever he could.

After he'd rested, he got to his feet and carried on walking again. As he passed the butcher shop, Mr. Mills the butcher was standing in the doorway talking to two women who had their backs to Will. "Hello Will!" called the butcher. When the women turned and saw Will, one of them said, "Hello, Will, shouldn't you be up west working in the House?" Will stopped and recognising that the woman was teasing said, "I'm not needed there today, Gracie, but rest assured that as always I am on official business." He tipped his hat, smiling. "Now if you'll excuse me, I have that business to attend to."

He continued walking along Upper North Street and then crossed over to be on the side of the street where his first point of business was located, but as he walked he began to feel an uneasiness about him, although he couldn't at first put his finger on what was wrong. The feeling of uneasiness grew stronger until at last he realised that he could actually hear the cause of his unease. A whirring, buzzing sound was getting louder, although he still couldn't place where it was coming from.

It wasn't until he noticed a woman on the other side of the street looking up into the sky that he realised that the sound was actually coming from above. Looking up, he saw what looked like giant silver dragonflies in the hazy blue sky, but which were in fact German Gotha bombers. Will and the woman across the street stood staring at the scene above in silence, neither of them quite realising what was happening, or aware of the threat that the planes carried. There had already been bombing raids by the Germans during the war of course, but these had always been done at night and been carried out by zeppelin airships, so the sight of these planes above the East End in broad daylight was a new and confusing sight.

Above the now distinct buzz of the plane's engines, Will could now detect another sound; a whistling noise that was getting louder and closer.

"Get down!" he yelled to the woman on the other side of the street. Will threw himself to the ground as did the woman and no sooner had they done this than there was a mighty explosion that shook them and the buildings around them. The next thing he heard shook him to the very core of his soul. The woman across the street began to wail. "The school!" she screamed. Will looked up and couldn't believe the sight that beheld his eyes. The infant school ahead of him had taken a direct hit. He scrambled to his feet and shaking and stumbling he forced his old and tired legs towards the school as fast as they would move. Other people were now coming out of nearby houses and shops and were running towards the school too.

Stunned children were beginning to stumble out of the school, some limping, some clearly in shock, many bloodied. Then the sound of hysterical children crying filled the air. When Will reached the school he was gasping for breath from running. Dust now filled the air too, making it even harder for him to breathe. He stumbled forward into the school building and began looking for children to help. The first child that he came across was a small girl that was lying on the ground cradling her arm and crying. He gently helped her to her feet and led her outside. Her tear covered damp face was white from the dust that had stuck to it.

He led her away from the school to a spot where the other stunned children were being gathered together. Will left her there with the others and then re-entered the school where he spotted two disoriented boys trying to find their way through the rubble. "This way boys!" he called out. The confused boys made their way to Will and he took their tiny hands in his and led them outside. For a moment the smallness of their hands in his made his stomach turn. It was a stark reminder of just how young and innocent the victims of this horror were.

"It's all over boys," he said, trying to comfort them. "We'll soon get you home to your parents."

When they were safely out of the school and with the other rescued children, Will quickly turned and headed back inside, passing other rescuers as they helped children out of the smouldering building. Back inside, Will came across a woman that was covered in blood and dust; she was one of the teachers and she was clawing through some rubble and broken furniture. When she heard Will approach she cried, "There's someone under here!" Will bent down and helped her lift the rubble out of the way. A child groaned, but was still alive. Between them they lifted the young boy up and the teacher carried him outside. Will looked back down amongst the debris to see if he could see any other signs of life. His eyes found a tiny, dust covered hand sticking out from the rubble. "Can I get some help here?" he called urgently. Two men that had newly arrived on the scene came to his aid. They all began lifting the rubble, but it soon became apparent that the small child was beyond help. When they had freed her body, Will lifted the dead child and carried her outside, leaving the younger and stronger men to search through the rubble for any signs of life. To his dismay, other small bodies were also being carried out and placed on the pavement at the front of the school. He bent down and laid the small lifeless body next to four others that had already been placed there. When he tried to stand he was overcome; the emotion and pure horror of the situation was overwhelming. Luckily one of the men standing nearby held out his arm and steadied him. "Are you all right, Mr. Crooks?"

"Just give me a second and I'll be fine," Will said. He took out his handkerchief to mop his sweating brow. The heat of the day and the dust from the school meant that his handkerchief came away filthy. The young man stood around long enough to see that Will was all right and then he headed back towards the school. Will then followed close behind, half staggering back into the lower level. Two men were coming down the stairs carrying a bigger boy and his heart sank, but then the boy groaned and Will thanked god that he was still alive.

He stood looking up at the large hole in the ceiling as the others around him worked on all fours trying to find other children under the rubble. A woman covered in dust came to stand by his side. "I can barely take it all in, Mr. Crooks," she said, her voice shaking and with tears streaming down her dirty face.

"Neither can I," he replied, his voice no more than a whisper.

"I teach some of the girls up on the 3rd floor," the woman told him. "The bomb came in through the roof, crashed through the floor, passed through the second floor where the older boys were and then crashed through the floor again and detonated when it landed here. This is where the younger ones were," and then she covered her face and began to sob uncontrollably. Will put his arm around her shoulder and did his best to comfort her. As he did, he watched as another dead child was carried from the building. They were soon to learn that 18 children had been killed, 16 of them under 6 years old.

65

On November 11th, 1918, Armistice day, World War 1 came to an end, and a general election was set for the following month on December 14th. The election was going to be a history making one. Women were given the right to vote for the first time, although they only qualified to vote if they were over 30 years of age and women of property. The Act that had given women the vote was the 'Representation of the people Act'. The Bill was passed by an overwhelming majority, which shocked everyone, even the suffragette movement itself. In the years leading up to the election, suffragette leader Emmeline Pankhurst, called upon the suffragettes to halt their campaign of violence and disruption and support the government in the war effort in any way it could. The part played by women in the war was absolutely vital to the country.

Many believe that the government allowed women to vote as a reward for their vital and hard work during the war years, as women took on many of the jobs that were left vacant after the men that were originally doing them had gone to war.

On a historical level, therefore, this was a momentous occasion.

On a national level, the Labour Party was looking to improve on its 42 members elected in the last election.

On a local level, the last two elections in Woolwich had Will and his conservative rival separated by less than 300 votes each time. This Woolwich election, however, would see no repeat of that drama. The constituency of Woolwich had been split in two; Woolwich East and Woolwich West. Will stood for Woolwich East and was unopposed and so remained a Member of Parliament.

Being unopposed was a welcome development for Will who's health had deteriorated even more since the school bombing from the previous year. That event had deeply affected him. Now 66 years old, he was grateful, as was Elizabeth that he didn't have to go through a draining election campaign.

The election was a successful one for the Labour Party as they increased their seats in Parliament to 57.

66

1921

The preceding years had seen Will's health deteriorate steadily, although he still tried his best to meet the demands of his political life. He could now only speak in little more than a whisper, the booming voice that had once filled so many meeting halls and the House of Commons had long since gone. He was a very weak and tired man. On February 21st, Will announced his retirement from politics. His public service that he had dedicated most of his adult life to was now at an end. Just a few months later on June 5th, Will passed away. He was 69.

Elizabeth sat in the living room of the house in Gough Street, which she had shared with Will for over twenty five years, reading the many telegrams and messages of condolence. The family were also gathered there dressed for the funeral. They were awaiting the arrival of the hearse and the funeral cortege.

"This one is from the King and Queen, God bless them," Elizabeth told the gathering. A loud knock on the street door interrupted them.

"They're here," somebody called from the hallway.

Elizabeth led the family out through the street door and was greeted there by a policeman that removed his helmet and said, "Please accept my condolences, Mrs. Crooks."

"Thank you, constable," she replied.

She took his outstretched arm and he led her outside to the street. Directly in front of them stood the black horse drawn hearse carrying the coffin that held her husband. On either side of the hearse stood a line of policeman on foot acting as a guard of honour. Two large black horses stood patiently in front of the hearse. Behind them at the front of the carriage, the driver, sitting high up in the driver's seat had also removed his top hat as a mark of respect. Behind him, the top of the hearse was covered in colourful wreaths. The coffin, which lay inside the open sided carriage was also lined and covered in wreaths.

"It's beautiful," said Elizabeth, smiling. She turned and looked at the procession of carriages and cars that lined the street behind it. She gasped when she saw the line fill the entire street and then disappear around the corner. "Good gracious!" she exclaimed. "There's so many carriages and cars."

"66 I believe," said the constable. "Mr. Crooks was a special man," he added.

"Yes he was," she agreed.

As the constable led Elizabeth and the family to their waiting carriages, he said. "I've been told that last night 3000 people filed past the open casket to pay their last respects, and another 3000 did so this morning."

Visibly moved, all Elizabeth could say was, "God bless them."

When everyone had taken their places in their carriages, the funeral procession moved off and headed the two miles to Tower Hamlets cemetery. The line of policemen that walked alongside the hearse were now joined by lines of mourners.

Once they left Gough Street, the family saw the full scale of people's affection towards Will. Shops along the funeral route were closed, houses had their curtains drawn and flags were flying at half-mast. As the cortege passed them, the men and boys of Poplar doffed their hats and many women wept openly. The common people of Poplar that Will had dedicated his life to serving lined the streets in their thousands to say goodbye to their fallen hero; a Poplar man that was born one of them, and not only remained one of them, but gave his life to serving them, no matter what their standing in life.

Following the funeral, after Elizabeth and the family had left, there followed a long procession of mourners that filed past the open grave, many dropping flowers and posies onto the coffin.

His gravestone read:

WILL CROOKS
AFTER A LIFE OF
LOVING SERVICE TO THE
NATION
PASSED FROM US ON JUNE 5th 1921
AGED 69 YEARS

A COOPER BY TRADE, HE BECAME
A GUARDIAN OF THE POOR
A BOROUGH COUNCILLOR
A MAYOR OF POPLAR
A LONDON COUNTY COUNCILLOR
A MEMBER OF PARLIAMENT
A PRIVY COUNCILLOR

He lived and died
a servant of the people.

The End

Printed in Great Britain
by Amazon.co.uk, Ltd.,
Marston Gate.